In memory of my grandfather, Chong Qui Cam, who supported every adventure I embarked on.

Plant
Society

Create an indoor oasis
for your urban space

Plant
Society

Create an indoor oasis
for your urban space

Jason Chongue

hardie grant books

Contents

A life with plants

My plant journey began with a lamb's ear (*Stachys byzantina*) I brought home from primary school in a tin. I was obsessed with it. It sparked my passion for gardening and as a child I would often sneak off on foot or the bus to explore the local nurseries, returning with a backpack full of plants and as many ceramic pots as I could carry.

Plants mean the world to me; there is something therapeutic and calming about their presence and they breathe life into every corner of my home. I have greenery draped over shelves and some of my houseplants are so large they almost touch the ceiling. I often need to prune leaves just so my partner and I can walk through the house.

My collection of plants has continuously evolved into my personal urban oasis. It's a heavily layered oasis, indoors and out, which I like to enhance by 'borrowing landscapes'. I do this by using the greenery surrounding my home – a neighbour's garden or a distant tree – to connect this indoor oasis with plants outdoors.

We often forget the need for greenery in our lives. As an architect and interior designer, I appreciate the importance of plants in a created space. They soothe harsh lines and blur the boundaries between one surface and another. I consider them a relationship between what we create and where we come from; a connection with earth. Plants remind us that our living spaces rely on more than man-made elements.

Houseplants are more than just objects. They invigorate our homes and spaces by filtering toxins in the air, replenishing oxygen levels and introducing a change in atmosphere. They also breathe life into our daily routine. My typical day is jam-packed, but I always find time for my plants. I've never been good at sleeping in so my days begin at 6 am, even on weekends! I'll get up early and walk our rescue dog, Ingrid, around Abbotsford Convent – an arts and community hub on the site of a former convent in inner Melbourne – then spend an hour tending to the plants. It might be just a quick water or prune before I get ready for work, but I find it a relaxing way to kick off the day. When the workday is done, I'm back watering and tidying in the garden or greenhouse before sitting down for dinner. On the weekend, I can lose hours among the foliage.

Although I grow a range of plant types, I instinctively sway towards tropical varieties as I find it easier to recreate their ideal microclimate indoors.

A tropical rainforest is a complex environment with a multitude of conditions – some areas are well lit, some have dappled light and the soil ranges from boggy to dry.

TROPICAL PLANTS ARE EXCELLENT CHOICES
FOR INDOOR GREENERY; YOU WILL BE ABLE
TO FIND A PLANT TO SUIT ALL LIGHT
CONDITIONS IN YOUR HOME.

However, most of these conditions can be easily replicated inside the home, allowing you to create your own indoor tropical oasis.

There is a tropical plant to suit almost any light intensity or soil condition, and with such an immense range of foliage textures and colour, they have endless styling potential in the home. But before you rush out to the nursery, it's important to understand that a healthy relationship with houseplants is based on patience, commitment and regular care and attention. In return for our patience, our plants reward us by making us happy as we gasp at their beauty and admire how they adapt to our built spaces.

I wrote this book because I want to share my love and enthusiasm for growing plants indoors, but most importantly, I want to show that it doesn't take much to create your own green spaces at home. I hope it inspires you to start your own personal plant journey.

A plant community

PRESERVING PLANT KNOWLEDGE AND SKILLS
INTO THE FUTURE

Indoor gardening was a prolific hobby in the 1950s, '60s and '70s, when greenery grew rampant through homes, rubber plants pressed up against ceilings and *Monstera* were left to grow wild in pots and indoor garden beds. But I've always believed gardening skipped a generation in the '80s. Basic gardening skills were not passed down and many houseplants are now rare due to a lack of appreciation and propagation.

I remember my childhood being filled with greenery. I'd spend hours gardening with my parents and grandparents, experimenting with whatever I could grow. Inspired by illustrated gardening books and shows like *Gardening Australia* and *Burke's Backyard*, I would plant seeds and cuttings and teach myself how to propagate, challenging myself with difficult methods like air layering. Growing up, I thought it was normal to garden for hours on end, but I now realise it was a rare experience and one I value greatly.

The life of a gardener is one of continuous patience and diligence. We constantly need to remind ourselves that plants take time to develop – they don't grow overnight. Even today, I still learn new tips and tricks from the growers and collectors I meet.

My love of plants led me to create The Plant Society (www.theplantsociety.com.au) in August 2016 with my partner, Nathan Smith. Nathan is an international flight attendant and because of his transient career, most of his life is spent in sterile spaces like planes, airports and hotel rooms, so he appreciates being home. Before we moved in together, he couldn't have plants or pets as he wasn't home all the time to give them the care they required. He now allows plants to grow around him and appreciates the calmness they create. Witnessing Nathan's growing fondness of plants has highlighted to me the restorative value they can have in our lives.

Nathan and I established The Plant Society to embrace our passion, but also to create a plant community, or as we like to call it, a 'plant social network'. Our goal is to nurture and preserve rare and interesting plant species for future generations and share the knowledge and skills required to grow them with our community. By celebrating plants and all things green, we hope to establish a knowledge bank of skills and techniques that can be enjoyed by all plant enthusiasts, whatever their skill level.

At The Plant Society, we believe it is vital to build relationships not only with the plants, but with the people who grow and nurture them. I have immense appreciation and respect for the knowledge cultivated by growers, collectors and propagators, and Nathan and I regularly forage the country to build relationships with these important people. But the journey has just begun. As we travel around and meet experienced growers, we are faced with one challenge: time. The older generation holds so much plant knowledge that is crying out to be unearthed and kept alive for the future.

Nathan and I have met amazing growers, collectors, managers of public gardens and horticulturalists who have spent years perfecting their skills and growing plants they are passionate about. Our conversations with these plant lovers have provided interesting insights into different houseplant species and gardening practices.

We now want to encourage *you* to begin your indoor gardening adventure; to get your hands in soil and help us establish a new generation of growers and propagators. This book will give you the skills you need to start growing your own tropical houseplants and easily develop your basic gardening skills. The instructions, methods and styling tips in the book mostly apply to tropical plants but many are easily transferable to other plant types. Once you have more confidence you can branch out to your backyard or balcony.

Along the way, I hope you develop the same appreciation for plants as Nathan and I have in our lives.

Happy gardening!

PREVIOUS SPREAD: WITH NATHAN AND INGRID AT OUR PLANT-FILLED HOME.

LEFT: MY GRANDMA AND I OUTSIDE HER HOME. SHE GROWS VEGETABLES IN HER FRONT YARD AND ENCOURAGED ME TO GARDEN WHEN I WAS A CHILD.

CHAPTER ONE

It's not that difficult

I learnt how to care for plants early on in my life, largely thanks to my grandmother, who gave me plant cuttings from a very young age. I practised propagating and growing plants of all sorts. Some flourished and some didn't but whether they survived or not, I learnt to observe and understand what plants need. Sometimes they just need their own space, otherwise they shut down.

The message here is, don't give up just because you kill a plant. Even the most talented gardeners have regular casualties. I've certainly killed my fair share of plants, usually as a result of my tendency to overcare. In other words, I can be a bit heavy-handed with the watering can (I've even been scolded by a nursery owner in Los Angeles for overwatering my fiddle-leaf figs). But as every gardener knows, you live and learn from the casualties because they remind you never to deprive them again, or in my case, to deprive them a little more!

Indoor gardening is all about experimenting and continuous trial and error to see which plants will grow indoors. If we can mimic a microclimate, we can begin growing all kinds of plants in our homes.

Black thumb to green thumb

People often think great gardeners are born with a 'green thumb' but I like to think differently. As with any hobby, practice makes perfect; the more you do it, the simpler gardening becomes.

Budding plant enthusiasts should also learn from the community around them and take in tips and tricks for different plant types. You will need to think laterally when your houseplants aren't thriving. They may have a disease or pest that will require you to work out a cure, or they may not be getting enough natural light to grow. Throughout this book, I will share some of the skills my fellow plant enthusiasts have shared with me over the years. Once you develop the basics, the possibilities of indoor gardening are limitless.

WHEN IN DOUBT, THINK LIKE A PLANT

My biggest tip when caring for houseplants is to think about how they grow in their natural environment. Ask yourself: Where do they grow naturally? Are they from a desert, rainforest or swamp? Do they grow on trees or under a rainforest canopy? Do they grow in bark or soil? Do they like the heat or do they prefer the cold?

This will help you understand the conditions your houseplants require in your home. If you can mimic your plant's natural environment, you will be able to make it feel at home indoors. Follow this tip and you'll be creating your own indoor rainforest in no time.

LEFT: A GLIMPSE INTO OUR BACKYARD LOOKING ONTO THE GREENHOUSE. OUR PLANT COLLECTION EXTENDS FROM THE INSIDE OUT.

RIGHT: MY GRANDMA HAS ALWAYS GIVEN ME GARDENING ADVICE.

ABOVE: GARDENING CAN BE A FANTASTIC COMMUNAL ACTIVITY – THIS GARDEN WAS ESTABLISHED BY A GROUP OF FRIENDS IN A DISUSED COMMERCIAL GREENHOUSE. THEY HAVE TURNED IT INTO A VERITABLE RAINFOREST, COMPLETE WITH BANANA TREES AND PINEAPPLES.

RIGHT: SHARING KNOWLEDGE, AND TRADING PLANTS AND CUTTINGS, IS ONE OF MY FAVOURITE ASPECTS OF LIVING WITH PLANTS.

Choosing the right plant for you

Gardening is about knowing what you can handle and building on your skills. When choosing your first houseplant, start with something low-maintenance and forgiving while you develop your indoor gardening skills. I often tell budding plant enthusiasts to put down a difficult plant and pick up what I call an 'icebreaker'. This will allow them to comfortably learn how to care for an indoor plant. From there, they can slowly build up their collection.

If you are new to the world of houseplants, it's important you choose the right first plant for you. Some of the best icebreaker varieties are peace lilies (*Spathiphyllum*), devil's ivy (*Epipremnum aureum*), cast-iron plant (*Aspidistra elatior*), Zanzibar gem (*Zamioculcas*) and fruit salad plant (*Monstera deliciosa*) (for more information, refer to the Plant encyclopedia on pages 67–99). These are all hardy varieties and will allow you to see and feel how they react to light, water and nutrition. Consider them your training wheels. Once they have helped you understand the basics, you'll be ready for more difficult plants.

If you're new to gardening, begin with one or two plants. A common mistake made by new plant enthusiasts is to buy plants for their entire home all in one go. This won't give you the time you need to establish the skills required for indoor gardening. Instead, start with one or two plants and use these to develop your skills. Once they are thriving and you've discovered what works, continue adding to your collection.

When choosing a plant at a nursery, ensure it is healthy and check it for pests and ailments. Look for wilted leaves or leaves with holes. Also check under the leaves as well as on branches and trunks for any pests that may have attached themselves to the plant. Squeeze the pot to ensure the root system is established. When squeezed, the pot should remain firm and the soil should stay intact. You can also gently pull the trunk up away from the soil while holding the pot in your hand to ensure the root system is established.

Always consider if it's the right time to buy a particular houseplant and try not to buy tropical plants in winter as they suffer from shock when exposed to cold temperatures. Similarly, if temperatures are high, be aware of the heat when transporting plants. Always remember plants need to acclimatise, so when you get them home, keep them sheltered from harsh light and strong draughts.

A great way to start your gardening journey is to exchange cuttings with other gardeners. This is an inexpensive way to practise with different types of plants.

It's always an experiment

Not every plant will work in your home. The reasons can range from temperature to light conditions. That's okay. Even the best plant enthusiasts struggle. Patience and experimentation go hand in hand when it comes to indoor gardening. I'm forever challenging myself with what I can grow indoors, and through experimentation I've learnt to grow a range of non-typical indoor plants, all of which have rewarded me with phenomenal foliage and flowers.

You have nothing to lose when trialling a plant indoors. It will either flourish or tell you it's not doing well. Either way, you will learn a positive lesson and over the years build up knowledge about which plants are best suited to your indoor environment. Consider it a mental diary of wins and losses, all of which contribute to making you a better gardener. There is really only one way to know if you can grow a plant in your home: give it a go! There are many things in life that should be feared, but growing indoor plants isn't one of them.

KEEP AN EYE OUT FOR PLANTS WITH AMAZING FOLIAGE
TO ADD TO YOUR COLLECTION.
  PICTURED: *BROWNEOPSIS UCAYALINA* (LEFT) AND LEOPARD PLANT
  (*FARFUGIUM JAPONICUM 'AUREOMACULATUM'*) (RIGHT).

LEFT: ALWAYS ENSURE THAT YOUR PLANTS ARE SAFE TO HAVE AROUND YOUR PETS.
RIGHT: NOWADAYS, INGRID AND OUR PLANTS COEXIST PEACEFULLY.

Plants and pets

Introducing plants around pets should be done with caution. Dogs and cats love to scratch and chew plants, which is upsetting for you, stressful for your plants and potentially toxic to your pets.

Our house was surrounded by concrete when we first moved in (the previous owner had sealed over the garden beds) and the only living thing was a cast-iron plant (*Aspidistra elatior*) in a vintage concrete pot. As soon as the first stage of renovations was over, we introduced some indoor plants. About the same time, we had adopted Ingrid, our rescue pup. One day, I was far too trusting and left her in the house while I was at work. When I returned, she had torn up the house, including my beloved plants! Thankfully they weren't toxic and I managed to save the trunks and replant them. Today, they are thriving again, and through some training, Ingrid knows not to chomp on them.

Many pets will become less interested in plants as they get older, but initially a little help is required to ensure they do not see your plants as toys. I leave Ingrid with a wide range of dog toys when she stays at home alone. This provides mental stimulation and teaches her to associate play with toys, not plants.

Some plants are harmful to your pets, so it's important to always check if a plant is safe around animals. Your local animal welfare association will have a list of non-toxic plants.

If you do have pets, good plants to add to your home include the radiator plant (*Peperomia*), prayer plant (*Maranta leuconeura*), African violet (*Saintpaulia*), zebra plant (*Aphelandra*), spider plant (*Chlorophytum comosum*), areca palm (*Dypsis lutescens*), aluminium plant (*Pilea cadierei*) and lipstick plant (*Aeschynanthus humilis*), but it's best to do your own research before introducing any houseplants to make sure they are safe for your pets.

Tools and materials

EVERY PLANT ENTHUSIAST NEEDS A GOOD TOOLKIT TO KEEP
THEIR PLANTS HAPPY AND TO MAKE MAINTENANCE EASIER.

AERATOR

Types: Plastic, metal, timber
Aerators are useful when you need to loosen
the soil around your plants. This is essential
for ensuring the soil isn't overly compacted and
allows nutrients, water and air to easily reach
the roots. I tend to use timber chopsticks from
takeaway stores; they work perfectly and are
completely free.

DUSTPAN AND BRUSH

Types: Plastic, metal, timber
Handy for the inevitable mess you'll create when
indoor gardening. Aesthetically, metal and timber
dustpans look best; however, plastic dustpans
will do the job.

GLOVES

Types: Plastic, canvas, leather
Gloves are important when gardening, to keep your
hands clean and to protect you from toxins in the
plant or soil that may irritate your skin. Disposable
plastic gloves are easier to move in and perfect for
fiddly and messy jobs such as repotting. Consider
purchasing some nice durable canvas gloves that
allow for long-term general use.

HAND TROWEL

Types: Plastic, metal, timber
A hand trowel is essential in your toolkit and will
be regularly used to dig up and transplant your
plants. It will also come in handy when you need
to aerate the soil in your pots.

Plastic trowels are the cheapest but a good metal
one with a timber handle is easier to dig with and
more durable. They have a nice weight, which
means less pressure on your hands.

MISTER

Types: Plastic, metal
To enhance the humidity around your plants and
simulate moisture in the air, you'll need a mister.
For something practical, you can purchase an
inexpensive plastic one, or for a designer mister,
go for brass or copper.

PLANT TIES

Types: Twine, plastic, metal wire
To train your plants to grow in a certain way,
you'll need ties to fasten your plants to a stake or
a trellis. Metal wire fasteners are longer lasting
and camouflage into the greenery.

SECATEURS

Types: Plastic, metal
A pair of secateurs is essential. You'll use these
regularly to prune and trim leaves and branches,
and to propagate. From experience, plastic-
handled secateurs break more easily, so I prefer
to spend a little more on a good-quality pair.

Keep them clean and sterilised by wiping or
rinsing off any excess soil or debris, then soak
them for ten minutes in a detergent solution
(1 cup dishwashing detergent to 4 litres [34 fl oz]
of water) to ensure diseases and pests aren't
transferred between plants. Rinse with water
after soaking.

SOIL SCOOP

Types: Plastic, metal
A soil scoop is rounder and more cylindrical
than a normal trowel and holds more soil at one
time when repotting plants. It allows for easier
scooping and backfilling of soil. Metal soil scoops
look great and last longer than plastic ones.

STAKES

Types: Plastic, metal, timber, bamboo
Stakes come in handy when your plants are a little lopsided or need some support. I use a combination of timber and metal, depending on the plant. If it is an enormous specimen, I like to use metal to ensure it can hold the weight of the plant for a long time, otherwise I like bamboo.

WATERING CAN

Types: Plastic, metal
There is nothing more important than a good watering can. I have two types in my toolkit, a large one with a spray-spout attachment for watering large plants (the spray spout allows you to rinse the leaves and clean off any dust that may be present) and a smaller one with a long narrow spout to get past the foliage and easily water at the base of plants on shelves or up high.

Plastic or metal are both good materials; however, you want to ensure a metal watering can stays free of rust. Personally, I find watering cans with a handle on the top easier to use, but you may find one with a handle at the back more comfortable to hold when full of water. In any case, make sure the spout pours freely – you want the water to flow from the watering can to your plants without dripping all over the floor.

Glossary

AERATOR
A tool for aerating soil and adding oxygen, water and nutrients.

AIR LAYERING
A propagation technique for propagating new trees or shrubs from branches still attached on the parent plant. The stem is wrapped with moist sphagnum moss or soil to promote root growth.

BACKFILL
Refilling the pot with soil once the plant has been placed back into the pot.

BOGGY
Wet or muddy soil. Naturally these conditions are found in swamps and marshland.

CLOCHE
A small transparent cover for protecting plants and encouraging optimal plant growth.

CULTIVARS
A plant variety produced through selective breeding.

CUTTING
A piece of a plant harvested from an established plant to create a new plant.

DAPPLED LIGHT
Natural light that has been filtered through the leaves of trees or through a window if indoors.

DIVISION
The act of separating a plant into multiple plants.

DORMANCY
A period where the plant slows growth to preserve energy for the growing season.

DRENCH
To soak the soil thoroughly.

HONEYDEW
A sweet, sticky substance left on leaves and branches by insects such as aphids.

LAYERING
Curating a collection of plants to create a visually appealing grouping of texture, colour and form.

LEAF CURL
A plant disease where the leaves curl in response to stress of natural diseases.

LEAF DROP
The falling of leaves at an accelerated rate usually caused by disease or too little, or too much, watering.

LEGGY
Long spindly growth occurring from lack of natural light.

MICROCLIMATE
A controlled climate that replicates a natural environment on a smaller scale.

NEEM OIL
A natural vegetable oil produced from the fruit and seed of the neem tree. Neem oil is regularly used for pest control.

NODE
The part of the plant where the petiole meets the stem of the plant. A node typically holds one or two leaves.

PEAT MOSS
Decomposed sphagnum moss. Used in potting mixes and soils to retain water and nutrients.

PERENNIAL
A perennial plant is one that lives for several years.

PERLITE
A white popcorn-like product used in horticulture to help aerate soil and improve drainage.

PETIOLE
The stalk that joins the leaf to the stem of the plant.

PHOTOSYNTHESIS
The process where plants use natural light to alter carbon dioxide and water to create oxygen.

PROPAGATE
Creating and multiplying plants from parent plants through a range of techniques.

ROOT BALL
The main mass of roots at the base of the plant.

ROOT BOUND
A condition where the plant's root system is confined and the roots become densely tangled within the pot.

ROOT ROT
A condition where the roots of a plant rot due to poor soil drainage and overwatering.

ROOTING AID/HORMONE
A product (either artificial or natural) that stimulates root growth in propagated cuttings.

SPHAGNUM MOSS
A natural moss used in gardening for its ability to store large quantities of water.

SPECIMEN PLANT
A rare or unusual plant that displays impressive foliage or form and is a focus in a room.

SUCKER
A shoot growing from the base or root of the plant that becomes a new plant.

TRAINING
Manually assisting a plant by using plant ties and stakes to direct the plant to grow a certain way.

VARIEGATION
Multi-coloured or patterned leaves or stems.

VERMICULITE
A natural mineral used in potting mix to enhance aeration and water drainage.

NAMING CONVENTIONS

Plant names can be confusing at the best of times. When it comes to naming plants, each plant is identified through a scientific naming convention specific to taxonomy. Plants are identified typically by Latin or Latinised words from other languages, beginning with family, genus and then species.

Consider the genus the generic name and the species name the specific name associated to the plant. Where plants have been hybridised or cultivated by humans, they will have a cultivar name usually assigned at the end of the plant's name. For the everyday, plants can also be identified by common or vernacular names. Common names are usually specific to country and location. Consider common names a plant's nickname.

Throughout this book, plants are referred to by their common name, genus and species. Within the Plant encyclopedia (pages 67–99), a range of alternative common names and varieties are also provided.

For example, the widely grown devil's ivy (*Epipremnum aureum*) will have the following naming convention:

COMMON NAME: devil's ivy
FAMILY: Araceae
GENUS: *Epipremnum*
SPECIES: *aureum*

Jeska & Dean Hearne

The Future Kept

LOCATION: SOUTH COAST, UNITED KINGDOM
OCCUPATION: PHOTOGRAPHERS AND LIFESTYLE STORE OWNERS
@THEFUTUREKEPT HTTPS://THEFUTUREKEPT.COM/

Jeska and Dean share a passion for curating homewares and lifestyle products to create beautiful interiors that have timeless qualities. They also have an immense appreciation for greenery. Jeska and Dean have managed to establish a 'working relationship' between their plants and their two cats.

PHOTOGRAPHS:JESKA & DEAN HEARNE

HOW MANY PLANTS ARE IN YOUR COLLECTION?
115.

WHAT DO PLANTS MEAN TO YOU?
Everything. We love to be surrounded by green at home and work. We filled our home with plants to create an indoor garden for all seasons as we can only really work on the outdoor garden for half of the year and on fair-weather days during winter.

WHAT TYPE OF PLANTS ARE YOU DRAWN TO AND WHY?
All kinds, we especially love our giant 16-year-old rubber plant, which was given to us by a local lady who was moving and had no room to take it with her. It is currently residing in the bathroom in the disused shower tray – while we renovate the kitchen!

TELL US ABOUT YOUR DAILY ROUTINE AND HOW PLANTS ARE INVOLVED.
We have filled our sunny home office with a mixture of cacti, succulents and trailing plants. We spend so much time in there that it's great to work with a backdrop of green. Having so many [plants], we need to keep an eye on certain ones daily. Some of the species with smaller leaves can dry out in a day if neglected; a lot of misting happens, and watering every few days in the warmer months.

HOW HAS YOUR PET LEARNT TO LIVE WITH PLANTS? ANY HORROR STORIES?
Apart from knocking a few [plants] over and occasionally taking out their rage on succulents when we leave on trips for too long, nibbling the ends of our ferns and giant aloe, [our cats] have been pretty good co-inhabitors.

WHAT CAME FIRST? PLANT OR PET?
The cats came first, the plants have slowly started to take over in the 4 years since we moved into our current home.

WHAT ARE YOUR FAVOURITE PET FRIENDLY PLANTS?
Ferns, *Haworthias* and *Tradescantia zebrina*.

CHAPTER TWO

A guide to indoor plants

I believe everyone should have plants in their home. They bring nature indoors and make a home calmer and more grounded. Gardening, whether indoors or outdoors, is also therapeutic and seeing your plants grow is extremely rewarding.

There is an incredible range of houseplants on offer in nurseries, allowing you to find a plant that suits your lifestyle and home environment. I'm a big fan of tropical plants – it's easy to simulate their natural environment indoors, and they can adapt to suit a range of spaces in your home.

Tropical houseplants

Most tropical houseplants originally come from rainforests, where they grow under large trees. In their natural environment, they crave warmer temperatures, humidity and dappled lighting. Luckily, these conditions can be easily replicated within our homes.

There is a huge range of colours, patterns, textures and shapes in the tropical plant family – some leaf forms still amaze me every time I look at them. Tropical plants also come in a variety of sizes to suit small or large spaces. You can easily build up a collection of smaller plants for an apartment or, if you have the space, cultivate a large feature plant to create impact. I have always had a soft spot for variegated (two-toned and patterned) leaves and rare and unusual plants.

Given the right conditions, tropical plants are highly adaptable. They effortlessly alter their growth habit to new light and temperature conditions and provide infinite fascination when their leaves form and open.

Not only do tropical plants display extraordinary foliage, they also help to remove a range of toxins from the air. Plants like devil's ivy, rubber plant and peace lily aid in removing formaldehyde, carbon dioxide and benzene from the air. In return, they provide fresh oxygen, making them perfect for bedrooms and living spaces.

TROPICAL PLANTS EASILY ADAPT INDOORS.
THEY CAN OCCUPY ANY SURFACE IN YOUR
HOME AND YOU CAN ARRANGE AND LAYER
THEM TO CREATE AN URBAN RAINFOREST.

Basic steps to healthy plants

Like humans, plants have basic requirements for survival. Light is important for your plants as an energy source and for stimulating photosynthesis, which converts sunlight into nutrients, while water and nutrition feed your plants and help them grow. If you can provide your plant with these three essentials, you'll be off to a good start. To be a good indoor gardener, think about your plant's needs and assess the conditions in your home to find the optimal spot for it.

A GREENHOUSE PROVIDES PERFECT GROWING CONDITIONS FOR TROPICAL PLANTS, BUT WITH THE RIGHT CARE, THEY WILL THRIVE IN YOUR APARTMENT AND HOME JUST AS WELL.

Light

Every plant requires a different level of lighting. By researching where it grows in its natural environment, you will be able to find a place in your home that best replicates a plant's optimum light conditions. Don't forget, plants are extremely adaptable, so don't panic if your home doesn't have the exact conditions you require. The trick is to watch how it responds in the first few days. If it wilts, develops brown edges or starts dropping leaves, it's probably not in the best position so move it to another location and keep watching it. When you notice the plant is responding well, the position you have chosen is perfect.

The right light

Lighting requirements differ greatly between plants, so it is important to observe the needs of each plant individually. As a general rule, tropical plants prefer indirect or 'dappled' lighting. Always observe the leaves of your plants. They will generally tell you if they are getting too much or too little light. For more information on specific lighting requirements of selected plants, refer to the Plant encyclopedia on pages 67–99.

1. HARSH LIGHT

Positioned close to windows that receive direct sun for most of the day. In the southern hemisphere, this would be north- or northeast-facing windows and in the northern hemisphere, south- or southwest-facing windows.

RECOMMENDED PLANTS/VARIETIES

Desert palms, kauri pines (*Agathis robusta*) and most succulents and cacti.

2. WELL LIT

Positioned in a place that receives several hours of direct sunlight throughout the day. An east- or west-facing window is perfect.

RECOMMENDED PLANTS/VARIETIES

Begonias, fiddle-leaf figs (*Ficus lyrata*), peace lilies (*Spathiphyllum*), radiator plants (*Peperomia*), wax plants (*Hoya*), zebra plants (*Aphelandra*).

3. DAPPLED LIGHT

Indirect sunlight sheltered by larger foliage, or positioned 2 to 3 metres (6.5 to 10 feet) away from windows.

RECOMMENDED PLANTS/VARIETIES

Arrowhead plants (*Syngonium*), bananas (*Musa*), Chinese evergreens (*Aglaonema*), Chinese money plants (*Pilea peperomioides*), *Monstera*, peace lilies (*Spathiphyllum*), *Philodendron*, pitcher plants (*Nepenthes*), prayer plants (*Maranta leuconeura*), queen of hearts (*Homalomena*), rubber plants (*Ficus elastica*), umbrella trees (*Schefflera*), zebra plants (*Aphelandra*) and most rainforest palms.

4. LOW LIGHT

Positioned in dark spaces such as bathrooms and rooms with minimal natural lighting or where windows are shaded by outdoor trees or obstructions.

RECOMMENDED PLANTS/VARIETIES

Bird's nest ferns (*Asplenium*), cast-iron plants (*Aspidistra elatior*), *Monstera*, paper plants (*Fatsia*), peace lilies (*Spathiphyllum*), *Philodendron*, Zanzibar gems (*Zamioculcas*), zebra plants (*Aphelandra*).

1

2

3

4

Watering

Watering is one of the most common things I get asked about when it comes to plants, but how much to water ultimately depends on what kind of plant it is and where it's positioned. If you know what to look for, your houseplants will usually tell you when they are thirsty. Common signs include wilting leaves, dry soil and leaf drop.

As a general guide, tropical houseplants like their potting medium kept moist in the warmer months, but ensure the soil dries out for a day or two between watering and only water again once the top 2 to 3 centimetres (¾ to 1¼ inches) are completely dry. Use your finger or a skewer to test the moisture level in the soil and avoid having your plants sit in water for more than a day. Decrease watering in winter but be careful of heaters – they can dry out your plant.

To avoid damage caused by artificial heating and cooling, make sure your plants are placed approximately 2 metres (6½ feet) away from a heating or cooling source. Misting your plants when the heater is on will also help preserve some moisture in the air. Most tropical plants love humidity, so misting can help promote growth and will keep leaves looking fresh.

WATERING IS ABOUT FINDING
THE RIGHT BALANCE BETWEEN
LETTING YOUR PLANT DRY OUT AND
REPLENISHING ITS MOISTURE LEVELS.

Soil and nutrition

When it comes to potted plants, it is vital they get the best nutrients from the potting medium they live in. Never use cheap potting mix or soil from the backyard. This will lead to problems from the get-go and handicap your plant's growth.

Indoor plants require a potting medium that isn't too compacted and dense, and that absorbs water easily. Always make sure your soil is rich with nutrients and appropriate for the type of plant you are growing. Unlike succulents, which prefer a gravel-based mix, tropical houseplants love good-quality potting mix that is lightweight, moisture-absorbent and free-draining.

Soil formulas

When repotting your tropical plants, it's important to choose the right base potting mix to allow your plants to thrive. Look for one that has been formulated for planting in containers and pots. When selecting a suitable potting mix, make sure the mixture is an equal combination of coarse and fine particles of bark and bark fibre. It should be moist, but not wet. When placed in your palm, the mix should move freely and not be clumpy or soggy. Avoid using potting mix with a large amount of gravel as it retains water when wet.

Good-quality potting mix is designed to retain moisture and nutrients and to allow air to get to the roots. Many plants will thrive off a good-quality store-bought potting mix. However, it's easy to make your own potting mixtures to suit specific plant species. On the following pages are a few easy recipes that suit a range of plants.

Mix your own soil

SOME HANDY TIPS FOR EASIER SOIL MIXING

TOOLS

Gardening bucket
Gloves
Measuring cup
Tablespoon
Trowel
Resealable container

- Mix your soil recipes in a clean gardening bucket to contain the mess and make it easier to stir the ingredients together.

- Wear gardening gloves to protect your hands and skin from any toxins in the soil.

- Mix soil on your laundry bench or outdoors on a workbench to avoid making a mess.

- If adding peat moss, soak it in a container of water for two days before mixing it into your soil recipe.

- Use a normal kitchen measuring cup and tablespoon to measure out ingredients but ensure they are only used for gardening.

- Ensure soil recipes are mixed evenly and adequately.

- Read the packaging instructions on fertiliser carefully, especially the sections about amounts for different plant types.

- Use a resealable container to store any excess soil.

Soil recipes

The ratios in the soil recipes below can easily be adapted or converted for larger quantities. Simply pour all the ingredients into a bucket and mix with your hands (make sure you use gloves) or a trowel.

General potting

PERFECT FOR THESE PLANTS/VARIETIES:

Dieffenbachia, Hoya, Monstera, Peperomia, Philodendron, Pilea.

WHAT YOU WILL NEED:

1 cup peat moss
1 cup premium potting mix
1 cup perlite
2 tbsp slow-release fertiliser

High moisture-retention plants

PERFECT FOR THESE PLANTS/VARIETIES:

Begonias, Chinese evergreens (*Aglaonema*), *Ficus*, peace lilies (*Spathiphyllum*), tassel ferns (*Huperzia*), zebra plants (*Aphelandra*).

WHAT YOU WILL NEED:

2 cups peat moss
1 cup premium potting mix
1 cup perlite
2 tbsp slow-release fertiliser

Low moisture-retention plants

PERFECT FOR THESE PLANTS/VARIETIES:

Sinningia, Hoffmania (also good for cacti and succulents).

WHAT YOU WILL NEED:

2 cups peat moss
1 cup perlite
1 cup coarse sand or gravel
2 tbsp slow-release fertiliser

Low moisture-retention tropical plants

PERFECT FOR THESE PLANTS/VARIETIES:

Hoya, Philodendron, Monstera, tail flower (*Anthurium*).

WHAT YOU WILL NEED:

2 cups premium-grade bark
1 cup premium potting mix
1 cup perlite
2 tbsp slow-release fertiliser

Propagating mix

PERFECT FOR:

Germinating seeds and propagating cuttings.

WHAT YOU WILL NEED:

1 cup peat moss
1 cup vermiculite

Feeding

After a couple of years your plant will have absorbed all the nutrients from the soil in its pot. The plant will become root bound and begin looking a little tired. Once the nutrients are gone, the plant may grow at a slower rate or begin dying back. These are signs that your plant may need more fertiliser.

All houseplants will benefit from being fertilised now and then. A combination of slow-release and liquid fertiliser aids in promoting growth and restoring nutrients for the plant to absorb. Slow-release fertiliser comes in the form of pellets or balls and provides controlled-release nutrition that typically lasts for months. On the other hand, liquid fertiliser is usually fish or seaweed-based and is typically diluted in water to provide plants with an instant feed.

The best time to feed your plants is in the growing season (generally spring and summer, but different climates may have longer or shorter seasons). For general base nutrients, mix a slow-release fertiliser through the soil, and in spring and summer, feed your plants with a liquid fertiliser to ensure they absorb the nutrients they need in the growing period. This will give them a helping hand and motivate them to grow faster and healthier. Always check the dosage rate for each plant type as some plants are more sensitive than others. The Plant encyclopedia on pages 67–99 has more specific information on fertilising requirements for different plants.

Temperature

Tropical plants vary in their temperature requirements but most prefer warm conditions between 15–30°C (60–85°F). Some can adapt to cooler temperatures of 10–20°C (50–70°F).

Refer to the table below for a general temperature guide for various plant species.

Cool-to-warm climate plants

COMMON NAME	BOTANICAL NAME
Maidenhair fern	*Adiantum*
Cast-iron plant	*Aspidistra elatior*
Spider plant	*Chlorophytum comosum*
Kangaroo vine	*Cissus antarctica*
Devil's ivy	*Epipremnum aureum*
Rubber plant	*Ficus elastica*
Nerve plant	*Fittonia*
Queen of hearts	*Homalomena*
Wax plant	*Hoya*
Prayer plant	*Maranta leuconeura*
Fruit salad plant	*Monstera deliciosa*
Radiator plant	*Peperomia*
Heart-leaved philodendron	*Philodendron cordatum*
Saddle-leaved plant	*Philodendron bipinnatifidum*
Aluminium plant	*Pilea cadierei*
Staghorn fern	*Platycerium*
Umbrella plant	*Schefflera*
Arrowhead plant	*Syngonium podophyllum*

Warm climate plants

COMMON NAME	BOTANICAL NAME
Lipstick plant	*Aeschynanthus pulcher*
Chinese evergreens	*Aglaonema*
Tail flower	*Anthurium*
Zebra plant	*Aphelandra*
Begonia	*Begonia*
Elephant ear	*Alocasia*
Peacock plant	*Calathea*
Dumb cane	*Dieffenbachia*
Dinner-plate ficus	*Ficus dammaropsis*
Mistletoe ficus	*Ficus deltoidea*
Fiddle-leaf fig	*Ficus lyrata*
Triangle ficus	*Ficus triangularis*
Tassel fern	*Huperzia*
Sensitive plant	*Mimosa pudica*
Swiss cheese vine	*Monstera obliqua*
Panda plant	*Philodendron bipennifolium*
Red emerald philodendron	*Philodendron* 'red emerald'
Chinese money plant	*Pilea peperomioides*
African violet	*Saintpaulia*
Peace lily	*Spathiphyllum*

Cleaning

Just like any surface in your home, houseplants collect dust, which over time blocks a leaf's pores and suffocates the plant. In their native habitat, plants are naturally cleaned by rain and wind, but since these forces are absent in our homes, indoor plants need a regular clean to keep them healthy. This maintenance is extremely important.

When you notice dust on the foliage of your plants, clean the leaves with a damp cloth or shower your plants in the bathroom to remove the dust and toxins sitting on the foliage. Yes, this literally means putting your plants in the shower and turning it on. This will allow your plants to breathe freely again.

While cleaning the foliage, also loosen the soil with a trowel or skewer. This will aerate the soil and reinvigorate the roots. It is also important to flush the soil with water every few months. Place the plant outside or in a sink and drench the soil so that water runs freely from the drainage holes. This aids in removing toxins in the soil and cleanses the root system.

On occasion, your houseplants will benefit from a visit to the outside world. Consider it a holiday for your plant friends. Sit them out on a balcony or in front of your home, but always check the weather first – it's important to acclimatise your plants and ensure they are protected from dramatic temperature changes, high winds and harsh sun. Remember, your plants normally live in a sheltered environment and are therefore more susceptible to being shocked by external conditions and get sun or wind burn.

With regular maintenance and optimum growing conditions, your indoor plants will stay healthy and flourish.

LEFT: A REGULAR SHOWER
LETS YOUR PLANTS BREATHE
FREELY AGAIN.

Choosing the right pot for your plant

When choosing a pot, consider watering requirements and where you want to position the plant in your home. Plastic pots are popular as they are better at conserving water. If using a clay or ceramic pot, make sure it is sealed to help preserve the moisture in the soil.

I prefer pots with drainage holes and a saucer to catch the water. However, if you fall in love with a pot without drainage holes, use it as a 'cover pot'. You can easily place a standard black plastic pot inside, making sure it isn't visible from the side. This will allow you to take the plant out for watering when required and let it freely drain. If the cover pot is too deep, line the bottom with pebbles before placing your plastic pot into it. This will provide drainage and ensure your plant isn't sitting directly in water.

1. PLASTIC POTS
The everyday plastic pot is great at conserving moisture.

2. CLAY POTS
Weathered terracotta pots are a classic. Make sure to seal them (with masonry sealer from the hardware store) so the soil does not dry out too fast.

3. CERAMIC POTS
Ceramic pots come in a wide range of styles and sizes. Keep an eye out for locally crafted pots.

4. GLASS POTS
Glass pots make interesting pots for growing plants in water.

Repotting different plant types

When plants are left in the same pot for too long they become root bound and can suffer from nutrient deficiency. Basically, the roots become tangled and stop the plant from growing healthily. When this happens, it is time to transfer the plant to a pot that will allow it to continue thriving.

Repotting is important for replacing nutrients and providing fresh drainage and aeration to the root system. As a general rule, it's a good idea to do a yearly repot of your houseplants. However, if your plants are still happy in their current pot, you can simply top up the plant with fresh soil mix. Over time though, your plants will extract all the nutrients from the potting mix so at some point you will need to repot to keep your plant happy.

WHEN TO REPOT

In the colder months, shorter days and less natural light will cause your houseplants to go into a dormant stage. Tropical plants naturally rest during this time to preserve their energy for growing in the warmer months. For this reason, the best time to repot is in spring or summer, when your plants are in their growing stage.

THERE ARE SEVERAL SIGNS YOUR PLANT MAY NEED TO BE REPOTTED:

- It begins to droop.

- It shows slow or leggy growth.

- The soil around the plant feels firm to the touch.

- Roots begin to grow through the drainage holes at the bottom of the pot.

THE RIGHT POT SIZE

It's vital to choose the right pot size when repotting your plants. Each time you repot your plants, move up to the next standard pot size. You don't want your plant to 'drown' in a pot that is too large. As a general tip, when choosing a replacement pot, try to allow 15 centimetres (6 inches) between the root ball of your plant and the edge of the pot.

How to repot

WHAT YOU WILL NEED:

Gloves
Skewer
Fork
Secateurs
Replacement pot
Trowel
Potting medium (see soil recipes
* on page 46)*
Slow-release fertiliser as required
* for your specific plant type.*

STEPS

1. Loosen the plant's root system in its existing pot. If it's in a plastic pot, press the sides to loosen the soil and root system. If it's in a ceramic or rigid pot, run a skewer around the sides to loosen the soil.

2. Remove the plant from its existing pot by placing your fingers around the trunk and over the soil surface. Flip the pot and plant upside down, allowing the plant to fall freely from the pot. You may need to gently tap the pot to help release the plant.

3. Gently loosen the roots with a fork, or use your fingers.

4. Trim approximately 2 cm (¾ in) off the root ball. This will help promote fresh roots and doesn't hurt the plant.

5. Place a layer of soil in your new pot along with a dose of slow-release fertiliser. Place your plant on the bed of soil so the top of the root ball sits approximately 1 to 2 cm (½ to ¾ in) below the rim of the pot.

6. Backfill with potting mix and fertilise with slow-release fertiliser as per the package instructions.

Pruning your plants

Houseplants benefit from a prune to shape them and to promote new growth. Pruning can help stimulate denser foliage if your plants become too leggy or if you want to keep a plant at a desired height.

The pruning techniques I use are pinch and secateur pruning.

Secateur pruning is perfect for removing large branches. Simply trim the branch back at the desired height or remove dead branches or diseased sections. Secateur pruning is used for drastic changes in your plant.

Pinch pruning is used to remove the tip of the plants. This technique is used to promote branching and is also great for controlling height. When plants are young, you can begin promoting denser growth by using this technique. Simply pinch the tip off the top of the plant with your fingernails, just above the leaf node.

For flowering plants, it is important to remove old flower buds. This is known as debudding. Once the flowers are spent, prune off the buds as close to the branch as possible. This promotes new flowers later on.

LEFT: PINCH PRUNING PROMOTES DENSER GROWTH.

RIGHT: SECATEUR-PRUNE YOUR PLANTS WHEN
THEY ARE GETTING TOO BIG. YOU CAN EASILY
PROPAGATE YOUR CUTTINGS.

Training your plants

Some plant enthusiasts like to let their plants grow wild, while others like to train them and control the growth and look of a plant. I love a mixture of wild and controlled, so my collection is a mixture of trained and untrained plants.

Training assists your plant in growing a certain way. Climbing and creeping houseplants like devil's ivy, *Philodendron* and wax plants, which grow up trees in the wild, will benefit from a support for them to attach to. Introducing a totem pole or support will allow your plants to attach onto a vertical surface. Some materials used for plant supports are tree-fern trunks, coconut fibre, and wire and timber trellises. When you first put these supports in the soil, you will need to attach the plant to the support with wire until they naturally grow onto it.

Plants that are outgrowing their spaces can be trimmed back to promote growth at a lower height. Simply determine the height you want the plant to be and prune back the branch. Plants like the rubber plant and fiddle-leaf fig benefit from pruning to control their height. Pruning tree-like plants also promotes branching, helps create more foliage density and gives the plant shape.

If your plants are growing lopsided and you want to straighten them, you can easily stake the branches to the desired position and allow the plant to establish in this form. Over time, the branch will harden and stay at the desired position.

LEFT: INITIALLY, YOUR PLANTS WILL NEED ASSISTANCE THROUGH TRAINING TO SHAPE THEM AND TO ENSURE THEY GROW IN A DESIRED WAY.

Christan Summers & Ivan Martinez

Tula House

LOCATION: BROOKYLN, NY, UNITED STATES OF AMERICA
OCCUPATION: CO-FOUNDERS OF TULA, PLANTS & DESIGN.
@TULAHOUSE HTTP://TULA.HOUSE/

Christan and Ivan are co-founders of Tula House. With Tulita, their mobile greenhouse, they promote plants and design throughout New York City. Their passion for plants doesn't end at work but is heavily intertwined with their daily routine, in an aim to celebrate the wonders of the natural world.

PHOTOGRAPHS: CHRISTAN SUMMERS & IVAN MARTINEZ

HOW MANY PLANTS ARE IN YOUR COLLECTION?

In our personal collection, I think we have around 20 plants. We have some big guys that we've been growing for years, plus a handful of odd specimens and rescues.

TELL US ABOUT YOUR DAILY ROUTINE AND HOW PLANTS ARE INVOLVED.

CS: Every morning we are woken at the crack of dawn by our lovely, very needy, cat, Nina, while her sister, Tina, watches quietly from afar. We've surrendered to the fact that it's a great substitute to an alarm clock. And from the moment we open our eyes, we see plants – from the night blooming cereus that gracefully hangs from a shelf above our bed to the 14-foot bird of paradise dominating our living space. I normally start the day with yoga and meditation, which has been a huge help to running the business and keeping stress and anxiety down. Ivan usually jumps right into the day's activity, his mom says he's just like his grandfather that way. From there, we tag-team the responsibilities of operating Tula, which is ever-changing. One day I could be at the nursery and tending to Tula plants where Ivan is cutting wood and making tables – the next we're immersed in computer work. The diversity of our days is one of the best parts of running a business.

IM: Seeing as we own a plant and design shop, we are surrounded by plants and greenery all day. Basically, everything we do is based upon plants in one way or another. I'm always researching and developing new designs for the health and maintenance of plants, as well as interesting objects, furniture and accessories that haven't been explored yet.

WHAT DRAWS YOU TO PLANTS?

CS: Their liveliness. Not in the sense that they're dancing around, but in the sense that they are alive and growing and ever-changing. Which I guess means they are dancing in very slow-motion. There is an innocence with plants and a profound truth in their nature of life. It's really touching for me.

IM: I grew up in Miami, so I think for me there is an underlying sense of nostalgia to home. Moving to New York was a shock as I had grown up with 20-foot bird of paradise plants in my backyard. Plants reintroduce a sense of well-being and comfort for me.

HOW HAS YOUR LIFE BENEFITED FROM GARDENING?

CS: I was taught to respect and appreciate Mother Nature through gardening and exploration at a young age, and that had a huge impact on who I am today. Before starting Tula, I was in working in advertising and without even realising that I was seeking some sort of sanctuary, I returned to indoor gardening. I would come home and care for my plants and little seedlings. I realised the peace that daily practice gave me and I would completely forget the daily stresses and even my exhaustion. I found a revitalised energy as soon as I got my hands dirty again and in these moments, [...] the idea of Tula began to grow.

HAVE YOU EVER KILLED A PLANT?

CS: Oh, yes! For sure. Overwatering, underwatering and lack of correct environment have all been culprits to plant deaths. I learn a lot from the mistakes and do my best to apply what I've learned moving forward.

IM: I have as well. When I first bought plants in New York, I didn't realise how harsh the indoor conditions would be for tropical plants. In particular, the uncontrollable heat in old New York buildings.

WHAT ARE YOUR TIPS WHEN IT COMES TO INDOOR GARDENING?

CS: Always consider your home environment first, then learn about the plant's environment to ensure you two are a match. Learn the name of your plants and research their origin. When you learn how and where plants grow and thrive, it changes the way you treat and care for them. A BIG tip is to always stick your finger into the soil before watering to make sure your plant friend is ready for that moisture. The largest culprit of indoor plant death is overwatering – so this will help you avoid that. Lastly, keep your green friends clean! Get a spray bottle or shower them under the faucet to rid them of dust and any hard-to-see pests. Since Mother Nature is not working her magic [indoors], we should clean the foliage [to help our plants] breathe better and ward away pests.

WHAT MADE YOU AND IVAN CREATE TULA HOUSE, AND TULITA?

CS: We love working with our hands – we love to create and build new and outlandish ideas. When we first started dating we would collaborate on small projects like concrete jewellery or photo essays. I fell into horticulture as an escape and in that I realised that advertising wasn't where I wanted to continue my career. Digging deeper into the plant world I discovered the opportunity for more education and curation – and Ivan began to uncover prospects in design. We quickly fell in love with the idea of a plant and design shop that innovates how city dwellers perceive the natural world – hence Tulita, our lovely plant truck. We also feel a transition happening, wherein people are seeking a connection to nature more and more. We hope that Tula will play a helpful role in that transition and guide people to interact and live with nature while respecting the history of horticulture.

WHAT ARE YOU MOST EXCITED ABOUT WHEN YOU THINK ABOUT PEOPLE LIVING WITH PLANTS?

IM: The possibilities that haven't been explored yet in what it means to live with plants. There's so much to go beyond a planter and a plant sitting in your room, and I'm intrigued by what we can do to push the boundaries by integrating home life and plants.

CS: People reconnecting to nature. I love, love, love receiving emails, calls visits, etc. from people reporting new growth, flowers, propagation – as well as plants that may be suffering. No matter the context, it means that those individuals are aware and paying attention to another life and that is so beyond exciting. I truly believe when we respectfully integrate the natural world, our daily lives will become healthier and richer with life.

CHAPTER THREE

Plant encyclopedia

The world of tropical houseplants is phenomenal. The huge range of plant types can be overwhelming for newcomers to indoor gardening, especially as care requirements differ between varieties. Even an avid plant enthusiast and true plant hunter can be baffled by a rare species.

This chapter gives a detailed overview of a number of tropical plants and their specific needs, from easy 'icebreaker' varieties to more difficult species. Whatever your skill level, this encyclopedia gives useful tips on how to care for your plant to ensure you can create the best possible conditions and enjoy it in all its beauty.

Arrowhead plant

DIFFICULTY
Easy
LEVEL

Syngonium podophyllum

ALTERNATIVE NAMES

Goosefoot plant, arrowhead vine, five fingers

LIGHT

Prefers bright indirect light.

WATER

Keep moist over the warmer months but not drenched. Reduce watering in the cooler months and allow the plant to dry out longer between watering.

NUTRIENTS

Feed with slow-release fertiliser once every six months (refer to packaging for dosage). In the warmer months, feed monthly with a liquid fertiliser.

IDEAL TEMPERATURE

Cool to warm

As its name suggests, the arrowhead plant has arrow-shaped foliage when young but as it matures, the leaves become more hand-like. This trailing vine is perfect in a hanging basket or left to trail over a shelf. The easy-care nature of this plant makes it perfect for a beginner.

Cast-iron plant

DIFFICULTY **Easy** LEVEL

Aspidistra elatior

COMMON VARIETIES

Elaitor variegata, Sichuanensis

LIGHT

Prefers low light.

WATER

Keep moist in warmer months but not drenched. Reduce watering in the cooler months and allow the plant to dry out longer between watering. Can adapt to dry conditions.

NUTRIENTS

Feed with slow-release fertiliser once every three months (refer to packaging for dosage). In the warmer months, feed every two months with a liquid fertiliser.

IDEAL TEMPERATURE

Cool to warm

Cast-iron plants are perfect for the beginner plant enthusiast as they are easy to care for and can adapt to low light levels. They have broad strappy leaves on long stalks and grow in clumps, making them great plants for layering amongst other plants.

Devil's ivy

Epipremnum aureum

ALTERNATIVE NAMES

Money plant, devil's vine, ivy arm, silver vine

COMMON VARIETIES

Marble queen, Frosty, Neon, Jade

LIGHT

Prefers indirect light but can adapt to low light.

WATER

Keep moist over the warmer months but not drenched. Water less in the cooler months and allow the soil to dry out longer between watering.

NUTRIENTS

Feed with slow-release fertiliser once every six months (refer to packaging for dosage). In the warmer months, feed twice with a liquid fertiliser.

IDEAL TEMPERATURE

Cool to warm

Devil's ivy is one of the most common houseplants available and is perfect for a beginner. It can handle a range of conditions and is forgiving if slightly neglected. Its glossy, heart-shaped leaves become variegated with yellow or white marbling and its long trailing growth makes it perfect for styling shelves, side tables or training up a pole or trellis. Devil's ivy suits a wide range of spaces and can be pruned back to control its size or to encourage denser growth.

Dumb cane

Dieffenbachia

DIFFICULTY · Easy · LEVEL

LIGHT

Prefers bright indirect light.

WATER

Water sparingly and keep mostly dry. Water once the surface of the soil looks dry.

NUTRIENTS

Feed with slow-release fertiliser once every six months (refer to packaging for dosage). In the warmer months feed every three months with a liquid fertiliser.

IDEAL TEMPERATURE

Warm

Dumb canes are perfect floor plants in your living room or study and show a wide range of patterning and colouring within the various cultivars. They have large, matt-textured broad leaves with thick stems and are a popular houseplant due to their easy-care nature.

Fruit salad plant

DIFFICULTY
Easy
LEVEL

Monstera deliciosa

ALTERNATIVE NAMES

Swiss cheese plant, monsterio delicio, Mexican breadfruit

VARIETIES

Borsigiana variegated

LIGHT

Prefers bright light but can adapt to low light.

WATER

Keep moist over the warmer months. Reduce watering in the cooler months and allow the plant to dry out longer between watering. Can adapt to drier conditions.

NUTRIENTS

Feed with slow-release fertiliser once every six months (refer to packaging for dosage). In the warmer months, feed monthly with a liquid fertiliser.

IDEAL TEMPERATURE

Cool to warm

The fruit salad plant is an enduring houseplant hero. When mature, its distinct, dark-green 'swiss cheese' leaf form creates a focal point for any interior. It can grow quite large or remain smaller when confined and its easy-care nature makes it a great plant for beginners. *Monstera* are perfect on shelves when small, but when they mature, they make perfect floor plants in living spaces.

Prayer plant

Maranta leuconeura

COMMON VARIETIES

Erythroneura, Kerchoveana

LIGHT

Prefers bright indirect light.

WATER

Keep moist over the warmer months but not soggy or waterlogged. Reduce watering in the cooler months and check on the soil frequently.

NUTRIENTS

Feed with slow-release fertiliser once every six months (refer to packaging for dosage). In the warmer months, feed fortnightly with a liquid fertiliser.

IDEAL TEMPERATURE

Cool to warm

Prayer plants have enchanting, moving foliage that closes at night and opens in the morning and its oval-shaped leaves have distinct red- or white-veined markings. This easy-care plant can be found as both small and large specimens, making it versatile when styling your home. Smaller plants can be placed on tables or on your bathroom vanity while larger plants are better suited to a desk or tabletop.

Peace lily

Spathiphyllum

ALTERNATIVE NAMES
Spath

COMMON VARIETIES
Wallisii, Domino, Picasso, Platinum, Sensation

LIGHT
Prefers bright indirect light.

WATER
Keep moist over the warmer months but not
drenched. Reduce watering in the cooler
months and allow the plant to dry out longer
between watering.

NUTRIENTS
Feed with slow-release fertiliser once every six
months (refer to packaging for dosage). In the
warmer months, feed fortnightly with a liquid
fertiliser.

IDEAL TEMPERATURE
Cool to warm

Peace lilies are extremely easy to care for and
perfect for the beginner. Their long, oval-shaped
ribbed leaves create an interesting upright plant.
Peace lilies are forgiving if slightly neglected
but when growing conditions are ideal they will
become lush green clumps of foliage with the
occasional white lily flower. They are perfect on the
floor to style a hallway, living or dining room.

Queen of hearts

Homalomena

COMMON VARIETIES

Rubescens, Maggie, Emerald gem, Wallisii

LIGHT

Prefers bright indirect light.

WATER

Keep moist over the warmer months but not soggy or waterlogged. Reduce watering in the cooler months and check on the soil frequently.

NUTRIENTS

Feed with slow-release fertiliser once every six months (refer to packaging for dosage). In the warmer months, feed fortnightly with a liquid fertiliser.

IDEAL TEMPERATURE

Warm

These plants have glossy heart-shaped leaves on the end of long red petioles. Some varieties have intense markings while others have simple, plain green leaves. This tall and slender houseplant can be easy-care or more difficult, depending on the variety. They are perfect for group planting on a tabletop or even your desk.

Rubber plant

Ficus elastica

ALTERNATIVE NAMES
Rubber bush, rubber tree, rubber fig

COMMON VARIETIES
Tineke, Burgundy, Ruby, Shrivereana, Lemon N Lime

LIGHT
Prefers indirect bright light but can adapt to low light.

WATER
Keep moist over the warmer months but not drenched. Water less in the cooler months and allow the soil to dry out longer between watering.

NUTRIENTS
Feed with slow-release fertiliser once every six months (refer to packaging for dosage). In the warmer months, feed monthly with a liquid fertiliser.

IDEAL TEMPERATURE
Cool to warm

The rubber plant is a popular large-specimen houseplant that draws enthusiasts with its rubbery, dark, glossy leaves. This easy-care plant can tolerate low-light conditions and slight neglect and its various cultivars offer a range of variegation and colour if you want to add some patterning to your interior. The rubber plant's large size is suited to larger spaces in your home where it can grow freely; it's perfect on your living room floor or in a double-height space such as a staircase void.

Swiss cheese vine

Monstera obliqua

ALTERNATIVE NAMES
Window leaf

LIGHT
Prefers bright light but can adapt to low light.

WATER
Keep moist over the warmer months. Reduce watering in the cooler months and allow the plant to dry out longer between watering. Can adapt to drier conditions.

NUTRIENTS
Feed with slow-release fertiliser once every six months (refer to packaging for dosage). In the warmer months, feed monthly with a liquid fertiliser.

IDEAL TEMPERATURE
Warm

The Swiss cheese vine is a rare relative of the fruit salad plant (*Monstera deliciosa*) and is highly sought after for its unusual leaf perforation and form, with dark-green leaves adorned with multiple holes. Its trailing growth makes it perfect for styling shelves or tabletops. It can be grown in hanging baskets or trained to grow up poles or screens.

Wax plant

Hoya

ALTERNATIVE NAMES

Wax vine, waxflower

COMMON VARIETIES

Carnosa, Australis, Linearis, Kerii, Obovata, Retusa

LIGHT

Prefers bright light.

WATER

Water sparingly and keep mostly dry.

NUTRIENTS

Feed with slow-release fertiliser once every six months (refer to packaging for dosage). In the warmer months, feed monthly with a liquid fertiliser.

IDEAL TEMPERATURE

Cool to warm

Wax plants come in a wide range of glossy leaf forms and colours and have a trailing or creeping nature. The immense variety of textures, sizes and shapes makes wax plants perfect for layering amongst other plants or curating a collection on a shelf or surface where their cascading foliage can be admired. They can also be trained to grow up a screen or trellis.

Zanzibar gem

Zamioculcas

ALTERNATIVE NAMES

ZZ plant

LIGHT

Prefers bright indirect light but can adapt to low light.

WATER

Water sparingly and keep mostly dry. Water once the surface of the soil looks dry.

NUTRIENTS

Feed with slow-release fertiliser once every six months (refer to packaging for dosage). In the warmer months, feed monthly with a liquid fertiliser.

IDEAL TEMPERATURE

Cool to warm

A Zanzibar gem is the perfect plant for a beginner as is extremely forgiving if slightly neglected. Its dark-green, shiny, waxy leaves look prehistoric, making it a great sculptural floor plant in your hallway or living room.

Begonia

Begonia

COMMON VARIETIES

Rex, Cane-stemmed, Angel wing, Tuberous

LIGHT

Prefers bright indirect light.

WATER

Keep moist over the warmer months but not soggy or waterlogged. Reduce watering in the cooler months and check on the soil frequently.

NUTRIENTS

Feed with slow-release fertiliser once every six months (refer to packaging for dosage). In the warmer months, feed fortnightly with a liquid fertiliser.

IDEAL TEMPERATURE

Warm

Begonias are the perfect plants for introducing bright colours into your houseplant collection and are perfect for styling on a floor or tabletop. There are hundreds of cultivars and for the avid grower they are a good challenge. Ensure good air circulation and a begonia will thrive and display intense foliage. Place them in a low position so you can look down and admire their foliage.

Radiator plant

Peperomia

COMMON VARIETIES

Caperata, Obtusifolia, Scandens, Argyreia, Prostrata

LIGHT

Prefers indirect bright light.

WATER

Water sparingly and keep mostly dry.

NUTRIENTS

Feed with slow-release fertiliser once every six months (refer to packaging for dosage). In the warmer months feed once every three months with a liquid fertiliser.

IDEAL TEMPERATURE

Warm

Radiator plants come in a range of shapes, colours and growth habits, making them versatile plants when it comes to styling a home. They grow into small plants indoors and typically have small, textured, heart-shaped leaves. They look great on a windowsill or tabletop, whether in groupings or alone. Water your peperomias sparingly; they prefer drier conditions and a good level of natural light.

Chinese money plant

Pilea peperomioides

ALTERNATIVE NAMES

Pancake plant, missionary plant, lefse plant

LIGHT

Prefers bright indirect light.

WATER

Keep moist over the warmer months. Reduce watering in the cooler months and allow the plant to dry out longer between watering.

NUTRIENTS

Feed with slow-release fertiliser once every six months (refer to packaging for dosage). In the warmer months, feed monthly with a liquid fertiliser.

IDEAL TEMPERATURE

Warm

The Chinese money plant has becomea highly desired variety throughout the world thanks to its almost perfectly round leaves that elegantly sit on the ends of long petioles. Chinese money plants thrive in bright indirect light and grow to approximately 50 centimetres (20 inches) tall and wide. These small- to medium-sized plants are perfect specimens to place on your dining table or sideboard to appreciate their beauty.

Dinner-plate ficus

Ficus dammaropsis

ALTERNATIVE NAMES
Kapiak, highland breadfruit

LIGHT
Prefers bright direct light to bright indirect light.

WATER
Keep moist over the warmer months. Reduce watering in the cooler months and allow the plant to dry out longer between watering.

NUTRIENTS
Feed with slow-release fertiliser once every six months (refer to packaging for dosage). In the warmer months, feed monthly with a liquid fertiliser.

IDEAL TEMPERATURE
Cool to warm

The dinner-plate ficus has one of the largest leaves of any houseplant. They have a bronze tinge when they first emerge before turning dark green and pleated, making this plant a spectacular specimen. This extremely rare tree is suitable as a floor plant in your living or dining room. It can grow quite large so make sure your space has enough height.

Peacock plant

Calathea

ALTERNATIVE NAMES

Zebra plant, rattlesnake plant

COMMON VARIETIES

Zebrina, Musaica, Orbifolia, Ornata, Makoyana

LIGHT

Prefers bright indirect light.

WATER

Keep moist over the warmer months but not soggy or waterlogged. Reduce watering in the cooler months and check on the soil frequently.

NUTRIENTS

Feed with slow-release fertiliser once every six months (refer to packaging for dosage). In the warmer months, feed fortnightly with a liquid fertiliser.

IDEAL TEMPERATURE

Warm

The wide range of patterning and textures in the *Calathea* genus vary greatly, so you're sure to find the perfect foliage to layer with in your home. Their vividly patterned leaves are typically oval shaped with strong leaf veining and marking. Peacock plants are best placed on the floor or tabletop. If placed at the right height, you'll easily see the brightly coloured underside of the leaves.

Tassel fern

DIFFICULTY
Medium
LEVEL

Huperzia

ALTERNATIVE NAMES
Firmosses, fir clubmosses

COMMON VARIETIES
Queensland, New Guinea, Philippine, American, Sensation

LIGHT
Prefers bright indirect light.

WATER
Keep moist over the warmer months but not drenched. Reduce watering in the cooler months and allow the plant to dry out longer between watering.

NUTRIENTS
Feed with slow-release fertiliser once every six months (refer to packaging for dosage). In the warmer months, feed monthly with a weak liquid fertiliser.

IDEAL TEMPERATURE
Warm

The tassel fern is a rare and unusual trailing plant that looks great on shelves or hanging from wall hooks. Ensure good air circulation and it will thrive. With a wide range of textures the tassel fern's foliage is fine and brush-like, with cascading growth. These soft and delicate plants make great specimens that soften hard surfaces within your home.

Maidenhair fern

DIFFICULTY

Hard

LEVEL

Adiantum

ALTERNATIVE NAMES

Walking fern

LIGHT

Prefers bright indirect light.

WATER

Keep moist at all times over the warmer months. Never allow the soil to dry out. Reduce watering in the cooler months and check on the soil frequently.

NUTRIENTS

Feed with slow-release fertiliser once every six months (refer to packaging for dosage). In the warmer months, feed fortnightly with a liquid fertiliser.

IDEAL TEMPERATURE

Cool to warm

Maidenhair ferns have graceful, fine leaves that overflow from their pots but, be warned, they are not the easiest plants to care for. If the soil is allowed to dry out, even for a short time, the foliage will dry and brown almost instantly. To avoid this, self-watering pots are perfect for ensuring they have an additional water source to feed from. Alternatively, place the pot on a bed of pebbles in a tray of water. Maidenhair ferns make great tabletop and floor plants.

Elephant ear

Alocasia

ALTERNATIVE NAMES

Kris plant

LIGHT

Prefers bright indirect light. Avoid direct light and low light.

WATER

Keep moist over the warmer months but not soggy or waterlogged. Reduce watering in the cooler months and check on the soil frequently.

NUTRIENTS

Feed with slow-release fertiliser once every six months (refer to packaging for dosage). In the warmer months, feed monthly with a liquid fertiliser. Do not feed when plant is dormant.

IDEAL TEMPERATURE

Warm

Elephant ears are a real gardener's plant and one of the most difficult indoor plants to care for. In the cooler months, an elephant ear will die back to its bulb in a growth stage called dormancy. Once the weather warms up it will spring back to life. There is a huge variety of unusual and interesting leaf shapes, forms and colours to this plant, making it perfect for styling on the floor or on a tabletop.

Fiddle-leaf fig

Ficus lyrata

ALTERNATIVE NAMES
Ficus pandurata

COMMON CULTIVARS
Bambino

LIGHT
Prefers indirect light with small amounts of direct light. Try placing your fiddle-leaf fig near a window that gets three to four hours of direct light per day and indirect light for the rest of the time.

WATER
Only water once the topsoil has dried (use your finger to check) and water sparingly – one cup every two weeks is enough, even in the warmer months. Reduce watering in the cooler months and allow the plant to dry out longer between drinks. About one cup, once a month, is enough in cold weather.

NUTRIENTS
Feed with a slow-release fertiliser once every six months (refer to packaging for dosage). In the warmer months, feed monthly with a liquid fertiliser.

IDEAL TEMPERATURE
Warm

The fiddle-leaf fig has enjoyed a resurgence recently, but as many have experienced, it isn't the easiest of plants to care for and requires a good source of natural light and warm temperatures. It can grow very large indoors and has beautiful violin-shaped leaves with strong veining. These specimen plants are perfect for styling in living spaces that allow them to be admired as large trees – try them on the floor in your dining or living room. Self-watering pots are perfect for keeping watering under control.

Tail flower

Anthurium

ALTERNATE NAMES
Laceleaf, painted tongue

LIGHT
Prefers bright indirect light.

WATER
Water sparingly and keep mostly dry. Water
once the surface of the soil looks dry.

NUTRIENTS
Feed with slow-release fertiliser once every six
months (refer to packaging for dosage). In the
warmer months, feed monthly with a liquid
fertiliser.

IDEAL TEMPERATURE
Warm

Tail flowers are predominantly grown for their waxy
flowers. Their remarkable range of foliage textures
and sizes make them superb specimen plants.
Some can grow quite large and are generally high
maintenance as they need to be kept warm. These
specimen plants are perfect for styling rooms where
you want something unique. The rarer species of
Anthurium are the most interesting in my opinion.

CHAPTER FOUR

Let's start multiplying

Gardening can get expensive if you only purchase plants from nurseries. I've adopted many of mine by trading cuttings with other gardeners or propagating my own. I've also inherited numerous cuttings from family, friends and neighbours. In fact, I rarely come home from a visit to a friend or family member without a handful of cuttings. We'll spend hours tending to their gardens while catching up on each other's lives and having a laugh. I'll help revive sick plants in their gardens and often receive cuttings as a reward for perking up their plants.

As a budding gardener, I taught myself how to propagate from books and gardening programs. I would plant every seed or fruit pip I could find and be in awe when they grew into trees and plants from the smallest thing. Whether rooting stem cuttings in water or dividing plants in soil, I still find so much joy in creating a new plant from another. There is nothing more satisfying than having your cutting strike roots and unfurl its first leaf. It still amazes me to this day. The only thing that brings me more joy is to pass on easy propagation methods to other gardeners.

Propagation basics

This chapter is a step-by-step beginner's guide to propagating your tropical houseplants and will help you practise a range of methods to propagate and grow your collection.

Unlike propagating succulents or cacti, which is as simple as picking off a leaf or stem and letting it grow a new plant, tropical varieties require a bit more work. However, with the right tips and tricks you will be growing new plants in no time.

WHEN TO PROPAGATE

The best time to propagate tropical houseplants is in the growing season (generally spring and summer but it may be shorter or longer in different climates). Warmer temperatures and increased sunlight heighten the chances of a cutting striking and establishing an adequate root system.

ROOTING MEDIUMS

Some tropical varieties can be easily propagated in water from stem, cane or leaf cuttings while others are propagated in soil via a method called 'division'. You can use rooting aid (also known as rooting hormone) to speed up the propagation time of your cuttings but it's not necessary. I prefer to allow the cutting to naturally strike as I love the process of gardening and enjoy taking it slow. If you do want to use rooting aid, it can be purchased from any good nursery.

POTTING ON

Potting on simply means planting a cutting in its own pot once it has established roots. Before potting on, ensure the root system is dense and has begun to branch out at numerous points so the cutting will thrive when transplanted into soil. Remember to select the right soil mix (see page 46) and appropriate pot size (see page 52) for your plant.

PROPAGATING VESSELS

Propagating and cultivating houseplants doesn't have to be drab. With the right vessel, your baby plants will add to the style of your home and a cutting can be given a personality of its own. From clay to glass, there are countless vessels you can propagate plants in and you can easily style your home with interesting shapes and forms that complement the plants you are cultivating.

Vessels for
water propagation

PROPAGATING IN WATER IS ONE OF THE EASIEST WAYS TO
MULTIPLY YOUR PLANTS. YOU CAN PROPAGATE IN EVERYDAY
OBJECTS SUCH AS DRINKING GLASSES, BUT YOU COULD ALSO
CONSIDER USING MORE STYLED VESSELS CRAFTED BY LOCAL
ARTISTS. AS LONG AS YOUR CUTTINGS ARE IN WATER, THEY
WILL DEVELOP IN A PROTECTED ENVIRONMENT.

To propagate using this method, simply place clean water into your vessel
and submerge the end of the cutting in water, but be sure to read the detailed
propagating instructions on pages 110–117 first.

1. CLEAR GLASS

Clear glass vessels are inexpensive and are
perfect if you would like to see the root system
develop. You can use jars or drinking glasses
from the kitchen, or get creative with vases or
even old laboratory equipment.

2. HANDMADE CERAMICS

A handmade ceramic vessel can give your cutting
its own personality. They can be found online
or through local markets or shops. The vast
selection of glazes and clay on offer can breathe
new life into your space. Ceramic vessels offer
more protection to your cutting's root system
than clear glass vessels; they also allow cuttings
to grow at a faster rate.

3. COLOURED GLASS

Old medicine jars and vintage bottles make great
coloured options for propagation vessels. The
coloured glass also protects the developing root
system and motivates it to grow faster. Find them
at vintage stores and flea markets.

4. DRINKING CUPS

If you run out of vessels to propagate in, you can
always resort to the regular cup or drinking glass.
They are perfect for holding multiple cuttings.

Vessels for soil and seed propagation

YOU CAN ALSO PROPAGATE DIRECTLY INTO SOIL, PARTICULARLY WHEN STARTING FROM SEED.

Most cuttings are small to begin with – select your vessel size accordingly. The range of available propagation vessels goes from inexpensive to stylish. I often let my cuttings establish in small black plastic pots before potting them up into handmade ceramic pieces. You can find small pots from nurseries, hardware stores and artist markets.

1.SMALL HANDMADE POTS

With a range of small handmade ceramic pots available, you can source the perfect size to plant your cuttings in. Keep an eye out for different textures and shapes.

2.CONCRETE

Concrete pots can be easily painted to personalise your cuttings and come in a range of sizes to suit large or small cuttings.

3.PLASTIC

Black plastic pots are the most cost-effective and are useful when you need to propagate a large number of plants. Try reusing old pots from other plants.

4.BONSAI PLANTERS

Bonsai planters are great shallow options for propagating. They are particularly good for seed propagation as their larger surface area allows for more seeds in the one container.

Indoor greenhouses

SOMETIMES HOUSEPLANTS NEED A HELPING HAND. GREENHOUSES,
MUCH LIKE TERRARIUMS, HELP TO ENHANCE THE GROWTH OF
TROPICAL PLANTS AND ASSIST WITH CREATING A MICROCLIMATE
AND MAINTAINING HUMIDITY.

A miniature greenhouse will promote growth and help establish propagated
cuttings fast. Consider them temporary terrariums that allow your smaller plants
to evolve into beautiful specimens. Some affordable indoor greenhouses include
a lidded jar or clear plastic bag. Others are more expensive but will be more
complementary to your interior style.

The following greenhouse types can be readily purchased from supermarkets,
local vintage stores or markets, or can be created from items you probably have
around the home. To maintain your greenhouse, you may need to mist inside it
every now and then to keep the humidity in the atmosphere. If your greenhouse
is looking a little dry, open it up and mist it once or twice. You can also leave the
lid open for an hour or two to provide some fresh air to circulate.

1. THRIFTY GREENHOUSE

Place your potted plant in the bottom of a clear
plastic freezer bag.

To keep the sides standing upright, place two or
three stakes (skewers work well) into the soil at
the edges of the pot.

Tie the top of the plastic bag with a tie or clip.

2. JAR GREENHOUSE

Place your potted plant on the bottom of a large
jar and close the lid. You can also do this upside
down – just put the potted plant on the lid of your
jar and screw the jar over your plant.

3. CLOCHE GREENHOUSE

Place your potted plant on a plate or tray. I like to
use one that is handmade and can collect water.
Once you have arranged your plant or plants,
place the glass cloche over your collection.

4. VASE GREENHOUSE

Find a transparent vase with a flat base large and
wide enough to hold your potted plants. Place
your potted plant inside and find a suitable lid
large enough to close the vase. The lid can be
transparent or solid, depending on the look you
are after.

5. DISPLAY-BOX GREENHOUSE

You can purchase these ready-to-go smaller
greenhouses from your local garden centre.
They make for easily accessible greenhouses for
plants that require regular maintenance. Simply
place your collection of plants into your lidded
greenhouse and close the lid.

Propagation techniques

Seeds and bulbs

PLANT TYPES

Oxalis, Alocasia

WHAT YOU NEED

*Seedling pots, or trays, full of propagating mix
   (see page 46)*
Seeds or bulbs
Clear plastic bag or glass cloche

STEPS

1. Plant a seed or bulb in your soil. How deep to plant
   the seed will depend on the type of plant you are
   propagating. Refer to the seed or bulb packaging
   for the depth required.

2. Water the soil mix thoroughly, ensuring it is drenched,
   but make sure the water can drain freely to avoid the
   pot sitting in water.

3. Enclose the pot or tray in a clear plastic bag or
   glass cloche.

4. Place the pot or tray on a bright windowsill that
   receives dappled or indirect light until the seed or
   bulb germinates.

5. Check on your seeds or bulbs every two days
   and make sure the soil stays moist. But don't
   overwater – the soil should be moist without the
   pot sitting in water.

6. Once your seeds and bulbs have established into
   seedlings you can pot them into their own pots.

Stem cutting

PLANT TYPES

Philodendron, Monstera, Ficus, Hoya

WHAT YOU NEED

Secateurs
Rooting aid/hormone (optional)
Propagating pots or tray filled with soil
(see page 46)

STEPS

1. Using your secateurs, cut a branch from a plant you want to prune – make sure it's a straight cut just below the node or leaf joint. Your cutting should have at least three nodes.

2. Using your secateurs again, remove two to three leaves from the bottom of the cutting.

3. Dip the bottom of the cutting in rooting hormone (if using) and place it into soil. Water the soil thoroughly, ensuring it is drenched, but allow the soil to drain to avoid the pot sitting in water.

4. You can also put the cutting directly into water and allow it to strike roots. It will be ready to plant into soil when it has developed a root system about 5 cm (2 in) or more in length. The longer you let your cutting's root system develop, the less likely it is to go into shock when transplanted.

5. Place your stem cutting on a bright windowsill that receives dappled light.

Leaf cutting

PLANT TYPES

Begonia, Peperomia, Saintpaulia

WHAT YOU NEED

Secateurs or scissors
Rooting aid/hormone (optional)
Propagating pots, or trays, filled with soil
  (see page 46)

STEPS

1. Using secateurs or scissors, trim off a healthy leaf close to the stem. Remove the petiole so only the leaf remains.

2. Dip the cut end into rooting hormone (if using).

3. Place the cut end partially into soil. Make sure the tip of the leaf cutting is above the soil's surface. Water the soil thoroughly, ensuring it is drenched, but allow the soil to drain to avoid the pot sitting in water.

4. Put your cutting on a bright windowsill that receives dappled light. It often helps to place the cutting in a mini greenhouse to speed up propagation.

Leaf petiole cutting

PLANT TYPES

Pilea, Begonia, Peperomia, Ficus

WHAT YOU NEED

Secateurs or scissors
Vessel of clean water

STEPS

1. Take a petiole cutting by trimming a leaf off the main plant. Ensure the petiole is still attached to the leaf.

2. Place the cut end into a vessel of clean water. Change the water every two weeks.

3. Place your cutting on a bright windowsill with dappled light to allow the plant to root. It will be ready to plant into soil when it has developed a root system approximately 5 cm (2 in) or more in length. The longer you let your cutting's root system develop, the less likely it is to go into shock when transplanted.

Leaf bud cutting

PLANT TYPES

Monstera, Epipremnum, Philodendron, Cissus

WHAT YOU NEED

Secateurs
Propagating pots, or trays, filled with soil
  (see page 46)

STEPS

1. Using your secateurs, take a cutting from your main plant by trimming a piece of the branch or stem between nodes. Make sure it's a straight cut and keep the leaf attached. You only require one node but you can propagate with more. Propagating with more nodes on the one cutting will create a more established plant.

2. Plant the cutting so that the stem sits horizontally under the soil's surface. Allow the remaining leaf / leaves to sit above the soil. Water your cutting so the soil is completely drenched. Allow the pot to drain freely and ensure the soil mixture is kept moist without the pot sitting in water.

3. Place on a bright windowsill in dappled light.

Leaf sectioning

PLANT TYPES

Begonia, Peperomia

WHAT YOU NEED

Scissors or secateurs
Sharp knife
Propagating pots, or trays, filled with soil
(see page 46)

STEPS

1. Select a large healthy leaf from the main plant.

2. Remove it at the petiole with some sharp secateurs or scissors.

3. Make wedge-shaped cuts through the leaf with a sharp knife, ensuring each wedge contains a central vein.

4. Place the central veined section into soil approximately 2 cm (¾ in) deep.

5. Water your cuttings so the soil is completely drenched. Allow the pot to drain freely and ensure the soil mixture is kept moist without the pot sitting in water.

6. Place on a bright windowsill in dappled light.

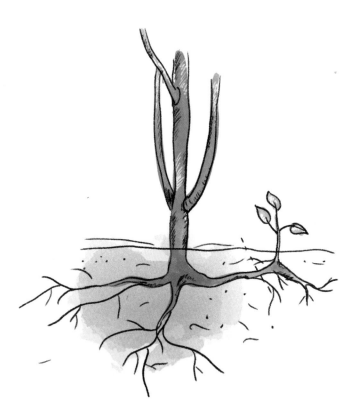

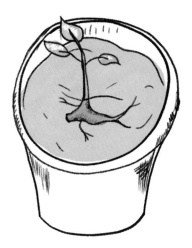

Suckers and runners

PLANT TYPES

Pilea, Chlorophytum

WHAT YOU NEED

Sharp knife/secateurs
New pot filled with propagating mix
(see page 46)

STEPS

1. Remove smaller offset plants from a mother plant by cutting the sucker at the base of the main plant with a knife or secateurs.

2. Suckers should only be removed once they have developed some mature leaves with a few evident roots at the base of the sucker.

3. Plant your suckers in propagating mix. Water them so the soil is completely drenched. Allow the pot to drain freely and ensure the soil mixture is kept moist without the pot sitting in water.

4. Put them somewhere that receives dappled light but keep them sheltered from extreme sunlight and wind. Once the root system has developed they can be repotted.

Division

PLANT TYPES

Spathiphyllum, Aspidistra

WHAT YOU NEED

Sharp knife
Trowel
New pot filled with soil (see page 46)

STEPS

1. Remove the plant you're dividing from its pot.

2. Separate the crown of the plant (the area where the stem joins the roots) into several groupings of plants. With a sharp knife or trowel, cut through the root and base of the plant leaving more than one plant in each divided group.

3. Plant the divided plants into pots as per the repotting tips on page 57. Water them so the soil is completely drenched. Allow the pot to drain freely and ensure the soil mixture is kept moist without the pot sitting in water.

4. Place the plants in an area that receives dappled light and protect them from hard winds and direct sunlight. Once the root system has developed and filled out the pot they can be potted up.

Charles Loh

Mossingarden

LOCATION: SINGAPORE
OCCUPATION: BOTANICAL ARTIST
@MOSSINGARDEN HTTP://MOSSINGARDEN.COM/

Small spaces pose no limit for greenery — botanical artist Charles Loh recreates nature in the smallest vessels and spaces, from terrariums to his plant-filled apartment. Charles aims to establish a balance with nature in all aspects of his life.

PHOTOGRAPHS: CHARLES LOH

HOW MANY PLANTS ARE IN YOUR COLLECTION?
60–70.

TELL US ABOUT YOUR DAILY ROUTINE AND HOW PLANTS ARE INVOLVED.
My start to the day usually involves having a slow-filtered coffee. I'll sit on the couch, enjoying the lights that come through my little studio. In the morning, before I begin any of my projects, I'll start observing my plants on the shelves to see if there's any new leaves from propagation, check for plant health and any unusual suspects like spidermite or root rot (because most of my plants are grown indoors, they tend to get these). I would sometimes head to the

nurseries to get supplies and hunt for new plants to adopt (it's never enough, even when I don't have much space left!). I do enjoy looking at [my plants] and observing the textures, colours and shapes. They are key to my works. The rest of the day will be spent thinking and brainstorming ideas and incorporating plant elements into my work.

WHAT DRAWS YOU TO PLANTS?

I was brought up in a city in urban Singapore, where typically greenery is everywhere. I meddled with aquascaping as a child, but I kind of lost [sight of] it growing up and eventually became a designer before turning to art full-time. I'm inspired by architecture and landscaping and how they coexist. Three years ago, I started experimenting with the idea of making my own terrarium and doing something hands on as a hobby, and I found plants amazingly able to adapt to their environments. [This sparked] my interest in plants.

WHAT WAS YOUR FIRST PLANT?

My first plant was the very old school yet popular *Monstera deliciosa*. I first noticed it when I did research on Henri Matisse, who had huge wild ones in his studio. I'm fascinated by the holes in the leaves that [make them] look like cheese (I found out it is also nicknamed Swiss-cheese plant). Eventually, it led me to keeping more tropical plants similar to its family.

HOW DID YOU LEARN ABOUT PROPAGATING YOUR PLANTS?

When I realised I've been keeping some hard-to-find plants, I wanted to multiply them to fill up the space I have. I read up on them online and asked the staff from the nursery how I can do that. The thing about 'plant people' is that they are always willing to share their experiences.

ANY TIPS FOR LOOKING AFTER HOUSEPLANTS?

Read up on the plant to check if it's suitable for your home (temperature, humidity and planting mediums are important) before committing to one [to avoid] killing it. Always find the right spot for the plant. Not all plants like direct sunlight; some prefer indirect filtered light. Look for signs of [poor] health (colour of the leaves, stems getting thinner etc.).

WHAT IS YOUR PLANT MAINTENANCE ROUTINE?

I keep mostly tropical houseplants and because I placed them all together, like a jungle, the humidity is high. So I only have to water them once every week.

CHAPTER FIVE

When things go wrong

Indoor gardening is a challenge at the best of times – things will go wrong and that's okay. It's easy to forget plants are a natural product, and sometimes nature just likes to make our lives interesting. When things go wrong, focus on how to solve the problem. Look for signs of change in foliage or soil and check if any pests are bothering the plant.

It's okay for your plants to be unhappy. Consider it a valuable lesson in how to respond to nature and refine your plants' microclimate. These lessons will add to your plant knowledge and over time you'll learn how to respond to changes in weather and climate. We can't stop our natural environment from changing but we can teach ourselves to respond to these changes promptly. Plants are extremely adaptable and will continuously surprise us by flourishing, even in less-than-optimal conditions.

Plant problems

The first thing to remember when you have plant problems is, don't panic! There is always a reason for your plant's unhappiness. It will often be over- or under-watering, poor-quality soil or poor air circulation. These factors weaken your plant's immune system and invite insects and disease in. But, where there's a problem, there's a solution.

SIGNS OF AN UNHAPPY PLANT

An important skill in gardening is observation. Your plants will talk to you when they are unhappy by displaying a number of telling signs. Looking for changes in your plant will help you identify symptoms and possible causes, and direct you to a solution. Look for a change in foliage, soil or growth habits. Pay attention to the mood of your plants and how they respond to changes in weather, light and air quality. Common houseplant problems often occur after a change in watering, light conditions, nutrition or temperature, or are linked to pests and diseases.

Keep track of how your plants looked when you first got them and they were healthy. If in doubt, compare your struggling plants to those of a friend. If your plants are a little sad, brainstorm the factors that could contribute to your plant's unhappiness and try to eliminate them. The trick with plant problems is to shortlist what may be wrong and address these problems one by one until your plant is happy again.

The list of common plant and pest problems on pages 126–133 will help you troubleshoot struggling plants and the Plant encyclopedia on pages 67–99 has information on specific plant types and their basic needs.

GENERAL PLANT MAINTENANCE FOR PROBLEM PLANTS

When your plants are looking sad, don't give up on them, give them extra love. Start by cleaning your unhappy plant and its surroundings (see page 51 for information on how to clean plants). A good clean will help to reinvigorate your plants and give them a fresh start. Remove dust and any insects that may be present. Regularly removing old leaves from the soil's surface will aid in minimising pests and diseases.

If a plant develops lopsided growth, rotate it regularly. Plants naturally grow towards the sunlight so rotation will promote even growth.

If a plant becomes diseased, prune back sick branches and leaves so the infection doesn't spread. I also like to treat the soil with neem oil or an equivalent natural pest and disease control. Always rinse or sterilise your tools when moving between sick and healthy plants to minimise the chances of contamination, and throw diseased or pest-ridden leaves and branches straight into the garbage. Do not compost them as this will spread the disease.

Unhappy plants can also be linked to poor air ventilation within your home. Houseplants require good airflow to reduce the risk of pests and diseases and to refresh stagnant air so, on a nice day, I recommend opening the windows and doors in your home to help bring in fresh air.

Homemade
pesticide and fungicide

When it comes to pest and disease control, I prefer to use natural methods. Before humans had ready access to chemicals, there was a whole array of natural homemade solutions to treat plant pests and diseases. Throughout history, we used natural oils and plants for this purpose. In India, for example, the oil and leaves of the neem tree have been used for centuries in cooking, cosmetics and as a natural pesticide.

Chilli pesticide recipe

WHAT YOU WILL NEED

4 cups water
1 tbsp chilli powder
6 drops dishwashing detergent
Spray bottle or mister

METHOD

1. Mix water, chilli powder and detergent directly in your spray bottle or mister.

2. Apply to the infected plant on a sunny day. Avoid applying in the evening or early mornings.

3. Spray directly onto the infected plant, ensuring all infected areas are covered in the solution.

4. Continue the treatment until all traces of pests are removed.

Neem oil pesticide recipe

WHAT YOU WILL NEED

4 cups water
1 tsp dishwashing detergent
2 tsp neem oil
Spray bottle or mister

METHOD

1. Mix water, detergent and neem oil directly in your spray bottle or mister.

2. Apply to the infected plant on a sunny day. Avoid applying in the evening or early mornings.

3. Spray directly onto the infected plant, ensuring all infected areas are covered in the solution.

4. Continue the treatment until all traces of pests are removed.

5. The recipe will still work without neem oil, but may not be as effective.

Organic fungicide recipe

WHAT YOU WILL NEED

4½ cups water
1 drop vegetable or neem oil
1 drop dishwashing detergent
2 tsp bicarbonate of soda (baking soda)
Spray bottle or mister

METHOD

1. Mix water, oil, detergent and the bicarbonate of soda directly in your spray bottle or mister.

2. Apply to the infected plant on a hot sunny day. Avoid evenings and early mornings.

3. Spray directly onto the infected plant ensuring all infected areas are covered in the solution.

4. Continue the treatment until all fungal traces are removed.

Identifying plant problems

Common plant problems relating to light

SYMPTOM	CAUSE	TIPS FOR SOLVING
Burnt foliage	Extreme sunlight on foliage.	Protect the plant from harsh sunlight in summer.
Leaf wilt	Heat and too much intense natural light.	Move the plant away from direct sunlight.
Leggy or thin growth	Not enough natural light.	Move the plant to a location with more intense natural light or longer light exposure.
Slow growth	Not enough natural light.	Move the plant to a location with more natural light or longer light exposure.
Yellow foliage and leaf drop	Too much natural light.	Move the plant away from intense direct sunlight.

Common plant problems relating to water

SYMPTOM	CAUSE	TIPS FOR SOLVING
Brown leaf edges	Dry air and not enough water.	Ensure the soil is kept moist.
Leaf drop or leaf curl	Too much or too little water. Can also be caused by too much liquid fertiliser in water or intense draughts drying out soil.	Ensure watering is adequate. Don't sit your plant in water and don't allow your plant to dry out for too long. Keep the plant away from draughts.
Root rot	Plant is sitting in water or watered too frequently.	Allow the plant to freely drain and avoid sitting it constantly in water.
Soil not absorbing water	Poor-quality soil.	Repot the plant into fresh, good-quality soil.

Common plant problems relating to temperature

SYMPTOM	CAUSE	TIPS FOR SOLVING
New leaves are too small	Temperature is too high.	Reduce the temperature or move the plant to a cooler spot.
Plant is growing too fast, causing deformed leaves (growing pains)	Temperature is not ideal for the plant.	Relocate the plant to cooler or warmer conditions as appropriate to the species.
Wilting	Temperature is too high.	Relocate the plant to a position with less direct sunlight and ensure it is adequately watered.
Yellow leaves, spots or bud drop	Temperature is too low.	Increase the temperature with artificial heating or relocate the plant to a warmer location.

Common plant problems relating to nutrients

SYMPTOM	CAUSE	TIPS FOR SOLVING
Slow growth	Lack of nutrients.	Apply a liquid or slow-release fertiliser and repot with good-quality soil if required.
Small leaves with yellow edges	Phosphorus deficiency.	Apply a liquid or slow-release fertiliser.
Stunted growth, small leaves and light–green leaves	Nitrogen deficiency.	Apply a liquid fertiliser or slow-release fertiliser.
Yellow edges that turn brown; affects bottom leaves first	Potassium deficiency.	Apply a liquid or slow-release fertiliser.
Yellow leaf but leaf veins remain green; new leaves affected first	Iron deficiency.	Apply liquid iron sulphate.

Common plant diseases

DISEASE	SYMPTOMS	CURE	PREVENTION
Bacterial blight	Small, pale-green blister-like spots on leaves that cause wilting.	Remove and dispose of infected leaves and treat the plant with natural fungicide. Avoid misting and reduce moisture on foliage.	Avoid excessive moisture on the foliage and ensure dead leaf debris is regularly removed from the surface of the soil. Make sure your plant has good air circulation.
Botrytis blight	Rotting brown leaves and stems with fuzzy grey spores during high humidity.	Trim off and dispose of infected leaves, stems and flowers.	Avoid excessive moisture in the air and in soil.
Crown rot	Wet, rotting roots that collapse and are black in colour. This soil-borne fungal disease likes wet soil. Foliage may yellow.	Drench soil with natural fungicide.	Ensure soil is free-draining and does not remain wet for extended periods of time. Allow soil to dry out between watering.
Leaf spot	Small circular yellow or brown irregular spots.	Remove and discard affected leaves and avoid misting. Spray with natural fungicide.	Ensure good air circulation around your plant and only mist when the air is hot and dry.

DISEASE	SYMPTOMS	CURE	PREVENTION
Sooty mould	Dusty black, sticky fungus that covers leaves, stems and branches. The fungus is usually the result of an insect infestation that secretes honeydew.	Treat insect infestation with natural pesticide and rub off fungus with soap and water.	Monitor for pests regularly and treat during early signs of infestation.
Powdery mildew	White-to-grey powdery fungal growth on the surface of leaves and occasionally on flower petals.	Spray with natural fungicide.	Ensure good air circulation and adequate natural lighting to your plant.

Common pests and antidotes

COMMON PEST	SYMPTOMS	CONTROL
Aphid	Small green or black insects that suck plant juices, especially new growth.	Use a mild soap and water mixture to remove aphids. Dilute a few teaspoons of detergent in a spray bottle and spray on affected areas. Alternatively, you can use neem oil pesticide (page 125).
Fungus gnats	Tiny black flying insects that thrive in constantly wet soil.	To treat adults, use sticky yellow insect traps (from your local supermarket, nursery or hardware store). To treat eggs in the soil, remove any decaying plant matter from the pot, then remove the top 2–5 cm (¾–2 in) of soil and discard it. Let the remaining soil dry out, then drench it with neem oil pesticide (page 125). Do multiple treatments, five days apart.
Mealy bug	Small insects with white hairs that feed on foliage, turning it yellow and causing it to die. They excrete a residue that can attract mould.	Spray infected areas with natural pesticide (page 125) and wash leaves.
Millipede	Millipedes feed on roots, bulbs and rhizomes and are found crawling in the soil or around your pots. These thin black critters are approximately 2–3 cm (¾–1¼ in) long.	Regularly remove old plant debris and keep the surrounding area clean. Treat with natural pesticide (page 125).

COMMON PEST	SYMPTOMS	CONTROL
Scale	Visible black bumps attached to leaves and branches. Causes plants to wilt, yellow and slowly die. Scale sometimes excrete sticky residue on leaves and trunks.	Pick off and gently scrub visible scale off leaves and branches. Alternatively, use an insecticide spray such as neem oil (see page 125), but be cautious when using natural insecticides on soft delicate leaves.
Snails and slugs	You'll see these slimy critters feeding on foliage, leaving a slimy trail.	Physically remove snails and slugs at night, making sure to look under foliage and pots. If required, use snail and slug bait but be careful around pets and children.
Spider mite	Reddish brown specks on foliage that feed off leaves, eventually turning leaves yellow.	Clean leaves with a mild soap and water mixture and treat with neem oil. Dilute a few teaspoons of detergent in water to wash leaves. Repeat in five days.
White fly	A small white fly that causes leaves to yellow and drop.	Spray with natural pesticide (page 125). Treat multiple times until the white flies aren't present anymore. Make sure treatments are five days apart.

India & Magnus

Haarkon

LOCATION: SHEFFIELD, UNITED KINGDOM
OCCUPATION: PHOTOGRAPHERS
@HAARKON_ HTTPS://WWW.HAARKON.CO.UK

India and Magnus live a life devoted to greenery. They travel the world and capture their plant adventures through photographs, shared on social media. Their passion for all things green extends into their home, which boasts an extensive collection of plants.

PHOTOGRAPHS: INDIA & MAGNUS

HOW MANY PLANTS ARE IN YOUR COLLECTION?
More than 100.

TELL US ABOUT YOUR DAILY ROUTINE AND HOW PLANTS ARE INVOLVED.
As photographers we don't really have much of a routine – each day brings something new and interesting. We spend a fair amount of time away from home, but always love to return and it's really important to us that our home is somewhere we love to be. Plants play a huge part in achieving that for us and they bring so much life and variation to our space. In all honesty, they don't take a huge amount of daily care – in fact they seem to thrive when we don't pay them so much attention!

WHAT DRAWS YOU TO PLANTS?
We love the richness in green foliage; it's a real connection to the outdoors and we really enjoy that we can provide a good environment for plants that would normally live all over the world. We tend to steer clear of plants that have bright colourful flowers and lean towards variety in the leaves. It's incredibly satisfying to watch them grow and change and they constantly surprise us with a new leaf or some strange unfolding tendril.

WHAT INSPIRED YOUR PASSION FOR GARDENING?
We fell into it, really – we love to spend time outdoors and began the Haarkon Greenhouse Tour to feed that interest. It's great to be able to travel the entire world inside one building by moving through different man-made climates. Visiting so many gardens and nurseries has meant that, inevitably, we brought plants home with us and we learnt how to look after them as an afterthought. We fell for them for their aesthetic first and foremost, but in order to maintain that and keep them looking great we had to learn about how to keep them healthy.

ANY TIPS FOR THE FIRST TIME GARDENER?
Get to know your home and what kind of environment it is. We have a light space without much direct light (in the summer at least), so our plants are quite happy. We'd always recommend that people do a bit of research into what a certain plant needs before they invest. Another good tip is to not give up at the first hurdle – sometimes it doesn't work out, but don't stop, persevere and find the right plant for your space and you'll be infinitely happy!

WHAT DO YOU LOOK FOR WHEN CHOOSING THE RIGHT PLANT?
Obviously it's important that we like the look of it. Our home is somewhere we have control over in terms of aesthetic and design and we have to see [the plant] all the time, so we know we need to love it. Now that we have so many plants, we have to make sure that a newcomer is exactly that and not just the same as another we already have – we're running out of space so we need to be careful!

WHAT PLANTS HAVE YOU BECOME OBSESSED WITH?
We have a couple of our own that we like to keep a close eye on: a *Pilea* that we check daily to see if it's decided to produce babies, and also a variegated *Monstera* that we got as a cutting from a friend – we also have a *Schefflera* that is constantly heading for the ceiling.

HAVE YOU EVER TRADED PLANTS AND WHAT DID YOU LOVE ABOUT IT?
Absolutely. Quite a few of our collection come from cuttings from friends and we are always propagating to give back to them – it's a great way of gaining new plants without having to buy them, it just requires a bit of patience!

CHAPTER SIX

Styling with plants

City living often means navigating a concrete jungle. Ever-increasing housing density means our homes are becoming smaller and smaller, and many of us now live in apartments and small spaces with limited access to, or views of, greenery. Now more than ever I believe that it is important not to lose sight of nature in our man-made spaces. Houseplants bring the outdoors inside and help visually lift our surroundings.

There is an immense range of plants to complement our living spaces. Whether you leave them to grow tall or place them to cascade over shelves, there is the perfect plant out there for every home.

When we moved into our little terrace house, it was surrounded by concrete. After renovating and creating a blank canvas, I began relocating houseplants that I had collected over the years from my parents' home to mine. Slowly but surely, I started to turn my house into an indoor rainforest. The plants are now the focus of our home and have created a microclimate of their own just minutes from the centre of Melbourne. I am so grateful that we live in an urban oasis and that plants have had such a positive effect on our lives. My houseplants connect me to the environment and blur the boundary between inside and out.

Softening hard surfaces

Throughout history, humans have used plants to breathe life into all sorts of spaces. Outdoors, we use them to beautify gardens, parks, streets and public spaces, including buildings – think shopping malls and office buildings. In our homes, houseplants add tranquillity, warmth and personality to even the coldest of rooms. Plants introduce organic shapes and colour into an environment otherwise dominated by hard surfaces and sharp edges.

With so many houseplants available, there is a never-ending list of options when introducing plants into your home. This chapter provides inspiration on how to create your own urban oasis. It guides you through connecting the indoors to the outside, choosing plants suited to the different rooms of your home and different types of furniture, and using pots in your interior styling.

Bringing the outdoors in

I've always believed our indoor lives should relate to our outdoor environment, and with living spaces becoming smaller, it is more vital than ever to appreciate our natural surroundings.

If you're fortunate enough to have views to a garden or other surrounding greenery, as I am, you can use these in your plant styling. This is called 'borrowed landscape' or 'borrowed scenery' and can extend the relationship between your indoor greenery and the world outside your window.

The art of borrowed landscape originated in China and Japan, where it was believed that by capturing a borrowed landscape within the context of a building, one could easily bring nature inside our man-made spaces. The practice links greenery in the foreground with views in the distance and was traditionally used to link external gardens to distant views.

We can easily use this practice to enhance the spaces we live in. Go to your window and look at the horizon. Look for interesting foliage, plants or trees and use them as inspiration when choosing indoor plants. Try complementing the textures and tones of your houseplants with ones in your borrowed landscape. Whether you have a small tree, a huge mountain or simply your neighbours' overflowing garden in the distance, you can create a strong relationship between inside and out by allowing that greenery to flow inside your home and become a borrowed landscape.

STYLING TIP: Connecting your indoor greenery with the outside can effectively make your interior feel bigger. To achieve this effect try styling your tabletops with smaller plants and using larger plants near windows to lead your eye towards the outdoors. Use the textures found in external greenery as inspiration for the plants you use indoors.

Layering with plant textures

A home can never have enough plants. As your plant collection grows, you'll find ways to start layering to create a little internal rainforest. Layering simply means curating a collection of plants to create a visually appealing grouping of texture, colour and form. The best thing about layering plants is that they can be appreciated as a group, but you also have little moments where you can appreciate the plants individually.

There are endless ways to layer your home with plants. I like to use natural environments, especially rainforests, for inspiration and I regularly rotate my plants between rooms and spaces. This allows my home to change and evolve with the plants I introduce.

When curating plants, always play with height, size and leaf texture to create interesting groupings. It's also good to create little 'plant families' by grouping your plants according to their light and watering needs. This makes caring for them easier. An example of a grouping with similar care needs is: peace lilies, fruit salad plants, Swiss cheese vines, devil's ivy and queen of hearts. Another good grouping is radiator plant, begonia, fiddle-leaf fig and peacock plant.

Choose a few plants to be the 'heroes' and complement them with plainer plants. For example, a variegated *Monstera*, with its unusually patterned leaves, should be the focus amongst plants with plainer foliage, such as a *Philodendron cordatum*.

STYLING TIP: Don't worry about having too many plants. Layering your plants with furniture and textiles can add depth to any room. A large grouping of houseplants helps to anchor your furniture. Here, I have played with a range of leaf forms and textures to soften a graphic rug.

Living room

The living room is the perfect place to go wild and use multiple plant types when styling. Use plants both individually and in groupings to get different effects. Tall, tree-like plants, like the rubber plant and dinner-plate ficus, are great specimen plants if you want to add drama into your room. You can also mix plain-leafed plants with more textured types.

GOOD PLANTS FOR THE LIVING ROOM

Bird of paradise (*Strelitzia nicolai*), devil's ivy (*Epipremnum aureum*), dinner-plate ficus (*Ficus dammaropsis*), fiddle-leaf fig (*Ficus lyrata*), fruit salad plant (*Monstera deliciosa*), *Medinilla magnifica,* peace lily (*Spathiphyllum*), *Philodendron,* queen of hearts (*Homalomena*), rubber plant (*Ficus elastica*), umbrella plant (*Schefflera*).

STYLING TIP: Play with a range of leaf textures to bring life into the dead corners of your living room. A mix of fine and broad leaves coupled with a seating arrangement can create a charming corner to read in.

PICTURED (FROM LEFT): DRAGON TREE (*DRACAENA*), ELEPHANT EAR (*ALOCASIA*), PEACE LILY (*STRATHIPHYLLUM* 'PICASSI').

PICTURED (FROM LEFT): FICUS ALII (*FICUS MACCELLANDII*), RADIATOR PLANT (*PEPEROMIA*), PONYTAIL PALM (*BEAUCARNEA RECURVATA*), UMBRELLA TREE (*SCHEFFLERA*).

STYLING TIP: If you don't want an indoor jungle but still want to incorporate greenery in your living room, try styling with a handful of plants. Smaller plants sit perfectly on your coffee table without blocking your view when seated on the sofa. Larger plants like Ficus Alii help to soften the harsh areas next to your sofa. When it comes to choosing pots, use similar textures and tones to those in your furniture to continue the style of your interior.

PICTURED (FROM LEFT): FRUIT SALAD PLANT (*MONSTERA DELICIOSA*), MISTLETOE CACTUS (*RHIPSALIS*), DEVIL'S IVY (*EPIPREMNUM AUREUM*), CHINESE MONEY PLANT (*PILEA PEPEROMIOIDES*), CTENANTHE, PEACE LILY (*SPATHIPHYLLUM* 'DOMINO').

STYLING TIP: If you love a dark palette, use plants with strong forms. Darker
coloured and more architectural leaves add depth to moody spaces. On the other
hand, a lighter space will make your plants stand out more. Whether you are
after a dark or light palette, let your plants spill out into your room. Use cascading
plants on windowsills and mantlepieces, tall upright growing plants on the floor
and smaller plants on coffee tables. When you build a bigger collection of plants,
start experimenting by layering with colour, texture, shape and size.

PICTURED (FROM LEFT): PEACOCK PLANT (*CALATHEA*), DUMB CANE (*DIEFFENBACHIA*)
CHINESE MONEY PLANT (*PILEA PEPEROMIOIDES*), RADIATOR PLANT (*PEPEROMIA*)
DEVIL'S IVY (*EPIPREMNUM AUREUM*), WAX PLANT (*HOYA*).

STYLING TIP: When you are not hosting dinner parties, plants can be your friends instead. Group a series of upright growing plants with different leaf shapes to create an interesting focus on the table. New and vintage pots can be combined in these groupings to add your personal style.

Dining room

There is nothing more special than having guests sit around your dinner table when it's adorned with some delicate plants. The best plants for your dining room are plants that will remain small and compact. There are several well-suited species with a range of colours and forms.

GOOD PLANTS FOR THE DINING ROOM

Begonia, Chinese money plant (*Pilea peperomioides*), peacock plant (*Calathea*), prayer plant (*Maranta leuconeura*), queen of hearts (*Homalomena*), radiator plant (*Peperomia*), wax plant (*Hoya*) .

STYLING TIP: Think about opportunities to tie the greenery on your dining table in with furniture nearby. Place draping, cascading plants on shelves to provide a connection to the smaller plants on your table. When selecting pots, draw inspiration from your interior. If you are a minimalist, try neutral-coloured pots.

PICTURED (ON SHELF, FROM LEFT): RADIATOR PLANT (*PEPEROMIA*), WAX PLANT (*HOYA*), WANDERING JEW (*TRADESCANTIA*), PEACOCK PLANT (*CALATHEA*), SWISS CHEESE VINE (*MONSTERA OBLIQUA*). ON TABLE FROM LEFT: QUEEN OF HEARTS (*HOMALOMENA* 'MAGGIE'), WATERMELON PEPEROMIA (*PEPEROMIA ARGYREIA*).

PICTURED: (LEFT) BOSTON FERN (*NEPHROLEPIS*), CANE BEGONIA, RADIATOR PLANT (*PEPEROMIA*).(RIGHT) SWISS CHEESE VINE (*MONSTERA OBLIQUA*), CHINESE MONEY PLANT (*PILEA PEPEROMIOIDES*), BEGONIA.

STYLING TIP: The dining table is the perfect spot to place the more temperamental plant species in your collection. Since you are frequently using this space, you will be motivated to check on your plants regularly. Style with smaller plants in handmade pots, so you can appreciate them up close.

Bedroom

We spend a large portion of our lives in our bedroom but it is often the last place we consider when introducing plants into our homes. Your bedside table is perfect for a compact plant that will help aerate the air while you sleep. Textural plants like devil's ivy, *Philodendron* and *Monstera* make a nice addition to your bedroom and are a great thing to look at when you first wake up.

GOOD BEDROOM PLANTS

Arrowhead plant (*Syngonium*), begonia, devil's ivy (*Epipremnum aureum*), fruit salad plant (*Monstera deliciosa*) peace lily (*Spathiphyllum*), rubber plant (*Ficus elastica*), wax plant (*Hoya*).

PICTURED: CANE BEGONIA

STYLING TIP: Even a single bedside plant can enrich your bedroom. If you like keeping your space minimal, choose a specimen plant with interesting foliage, such as variegated or patterned leaves. Use a pot that is neutral in colour so you don't detract from the plant.

PICTURED (FROM LEFT): LUCKY BAMBOO (*DRACAENA*), CARICA PAPAYA (*BABACO CARICA*),
DEVIL'S IVY (*EPIPREMNUM AUREUM*), CABBAGE TREE (*CUSSONIA*), CAST-IRON PLANT
(*ASPIDISTRA ELATIOR* 'SHOOTING STAR'), ZANZIBAR GEM (*ZAMIOCULCAS*).

STYLING TIP: Plants are great for styling in your bedroom. Use them alongside
beautiful bed linen to create a softer space. Delicate leaves will create beautiful
shadowing. Try incorporating interesting plant hangers to allow your plants to
drape down over your bed. Graphic pots are great for relating back to your artwork.

153

PICTURED (FROM LEFT): FIDDLE-LEAF FIG (*FICUS LYRATA* 'BAMBINI'), DEVIL'S IVY (*EPIPREMNUM AUREUM*), PEACOCK PLANT (*CALATHEA*), MISTLETOE CACTUS (*RHIPSALIS*).

STYLING TIP: Your spaces don't need to be white. Use plants to be playful and highlight colour. When you have a bold colour in your room, try complementing it with pots of a similar colour palette. Use plants to soften mantlepieces and place them on stands to add height to your space.

PICTURED (FROM LEFT): SNAKE PLANT
(*SANSEVIERIA*), WAX PLANT (*HOYA*),
FRUIT SALAD PLANT (*MONSTERA DELICIOSA*).

STYLING TIP: Plants can easily be integrated
into your bedroom. Don't forget to look for spots
where you might be able to hang plants.

STYLING TIP: If you have high ceilings, why not grow an indoor tree? Large foliage looks impressive when viewed from your bed, and smaller groupings of plants can add personality on your bedside table.

PICTURED (FROM LEFT): BIRD OF PARADISE (*STRELITZIA NICOLAI*), UMBRELLA PLANT (*SCHEFFLERA*).

PICTURED (FROM LEFT): BLUE STAR FERN (*PHLEBODIUM AUREUM*), DEVIL'S IVY (*EPIPREMNUM AUREUM*), WAX PLANT (*HOYA*), CTENANTHE.

STYLING TIP: Use the colours in your room as inspiration for the plants you grow. With the vast range of plant types available, you will easily find a plant to highlight the style in your bedroom. Consider using plants to fill bare spaces on your wall, and use taller floor plants to create height.

Bathroom

The bathroom is the perfect location for growing plants that love humidity. If you're short on space, try hanging devil's ivy or pitcher plants from shelves or the ceiling. Plants like peace lilies, queen of hearts and arrowhead plant are great for creating small groupings of plants placed next to your shower or beside your vanity.

GOOD BATHROOM PLANTS

Arrowhead plant (*Syngonium*), devil's ivy (*Epipremnum aureum*), peace lily (*Spathihyllum*), pitcher plant (*Nepenthes*), queen of hearts (*Homalomena*), tassel fern (*Huperzia*), zebra plant (*Aphelandra*).

PICTURED (FROM LEFT): DEVIL'S IVY (*EPIPREMNUM AUREUM*), WATERMELON VINE (*PELLIONIA*), WAX PLANT (*HOYA*), PEACE LILY (*SPATHIPHYLLUM* 'PICASSO').

STYLING TIP: Tropical plants typically love humidity. Place them on windowsills to allow them to grow downwards and soften the tiles. Additionally, you can place plants on the floor near your bathtub or shower. When styling harsh spaces I like to use natural fibres such as a woven basket to sit plants into.

PICTURED (FROM LEFT): ARROWHEAD PLANT (*SYNGONIUM*),
DEVIL'S IVY (*EPIPREMNUM AUREUM*).

STYLING TIP: Try using plants in your bathroom to bring
life into a typically cold space. Stools make perfect plant
stands and help to elevate your houseplants.

STYLING TIP: Plants can enhance the workplace. Suspending plants from the ceiling or placing them on desks are great ways to break up your office space. Use neutral coloured pots to avoid making the office too chaotic.

PICTURED (FROM LEFT): CTENANTHE, PHILODENDRON 'HOPE', HEART LEAF PHILODENDRON (*PHILODENDRON CORDATUM*), WEEPING FIG (*FICUS BENJAMINA*), DEVIL'S IVY (*EPIPREMNUM AUREUM*), FRUIT SALAD PLANT (*MONSTERA DELICIOSA*).

Office/Desk

Compact plants are perfect for decorating your desk at home or at the office. There is often limited natural light at work and air circulation is poor. Try using some hardier table plants such as the Zanzibar gem, cast-iron plant or peace lily.

GOOD OFFICE OR DESK PLANTS

Cast-iron plant (*Aspidistra elatior*), fruit salad plant (*Monstera deliciosa*), peace lily (*Spathihyllum*), Zanzibar gem (*Zamioculcas*).

STYLING TIP: Plants bring life to corners and dead spaces in the office. Training plants to grow up against the wall will help soften harsh lines.

PICTURED: FRUIT SALAD PLANT (*MONSTERA DELICIOSA*), BIRD'S NEST FERN (*ASPLENIUM*).

STYLING TIP: Cascading plants are great for sitting at the edge of shelves and voids.

PICTURED (LEFT): PEACOCK PLANT (*CALATHEA ORBIFOLIA*), SATIN POTHOS (*SCINDAPSUS PICTUS*), DEVIL'S IVY (*EPIPREMNUM AUREUM*). RIGHT: DEVIL'S IVY (*EPIPREMNUM AUREUM*), BLUE STAR FERN (*PHLEBODIUM AUREUM*).

STYLING TIP: Kitchenettes in offices are often forgotten when it comes to styling. Even when you are short on space, there are places you can incorporate greenery. Plants can be grown higher up, out of the way. Delicate leaves perfectly complement bold architectural features.

Meeting and reception areas

Plants make for a nice welcome when placed in hallways in your home and in reception spaces. They are comforting and create a calming first impression. These spaces are often used heavily and have limited natural lighting so try using plants like the cast-iron plant, rubber plant or umbrella tree.

GOOD HALLWAY, WAITING ROOM OR RECEPTION PLANTS

Bird of paradise (*Strelitzia nicolai*), cast-iron plant (*Aspidistra elatior*), dumb cane (*Dieffenbachia*), lady palm (*Rhapis*), rubber plant (*Ficus elastica*) .

STYLING TIP: Plants have a calming effect in waiting rooms. Consider grouping a number of plants to create a focal point. Smaller plants in handmade ceramic pots are perfect for side tables where they can be appreciated close up.

PICTURED: BIRD OF PARADISE (*STRELITZIA NICOLAI*), RUBBER PLANT (*FICUS ELASTICA*), BOSTON FERN (*NEPHROLEPIS*), PHILODENDRON, DEVIL'S IVY (*EPIPREMNUM AUREUM*), BLUE STAR FERN (*PHLEBODIUM AUREUM*).

PICTURED: SADDLE LEAFED PLANT (*PHILODENDRON BIPINNATIFIDUM*), CAST-IRON PLANT (*ASPIDISTRA ELATIOR*), BIRD OF PARADISE (*STRELITZIA NICOLAI*), FRUIT SALAD PLANT (*MONSTERA DELICIOSA*).

STYLING TIP: Meeting areas are typically lifeless and stark. Introducing larger plants around the meeting room can lighten the mood while also keeping the meeting table free for paperwork.

Styling with a range of plants

There is a vast range of plants which naturally suit different surfaces in your home. Some plants remain compact when mature, while others become tall trees. When styling with plants, observe their growth habits.

Working out whether a plant grows upright or cascades will help you decide on the right position for it in your home. Some plants naturally lend themselves to being placed on shelves while others require enough height to grow before they hit the ceiling. The following pages present a range of plants well suited to different areas in your home.

Floor plants

Chinese evergreen (*Aglaonema*), dinner-plate ficus (*Ficus dammaropsis*), dumb cane (*Dieffenbachia*), fiddle-leaf fig (*Ficus lyrata*), kauri pine (*Agathis robusta*), lucky bamboo (*Dracaena*), mistletoe ficus (*Ficus deltoidea*), peace lily (*Spathiphyllum*), peacock plant (*Calathea*), rubber plant (*Ficus elastica*), tail flower (*Anthurium*), umbrella plant (*Schefflera*) and plants from the *Monstera, Caladium* and *Bromeliad family*.

1 MISTLETOE FICUS (*Ficus deltoidea*)
Oval-shaped leaves and small figs make this an interesting specimen plant.

2 FRUIT SALAD PLANT (*Monstera deliciosa*)
If you are after impact, this much loved houseplant unfurls large split leaves (see page 72).

3 DUMB CANE (*Dieffenbachia*)
Adorned with variegated and patterned leaves, the dumb cane will add texture to any room (see page 71).

4 FIDDLE-LEAF FIG (*Ficus lyrata*)
With the right care, a fiddle-leaf fig makes for the perfect indoor tree (see page 96).

5 QUEEN OF HEARTS (*Homalomena*)
Elegant, heart-shaped leaves emerge from the crown to form a dense floor plant (see page 76).

Table plants

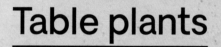

SMALL PLANTS THAT ADD LIFE TO YOUR TABLETOPS

Chinese money plant (*Pilea peperomioides*), peacock plant
(*Calathea*), prayer plant (*Maranta leuconeura*), watermelon
peperomia (*Peperomia agryreia*), wax plant (*Hoya*) and plants
from the asparagus fern family.

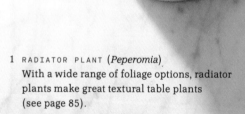

1 RADIATOR PLANT (*Peperomia*)
   With a wide range of foliage options, radiator
   plants make great textural table plants
   (see page 85).

2 TRACTOR SEAT PLANT (*Ligularia reniformis*)
   These glossy kidney-shaped leaves create the
   perfect simple backdrop when accompanied with
   a more colourful or textured plant.

3 WAX PLANT (*Hoya*)
   If you are wanting to soften the edge of your table
   try draping a wax flower plant on or over the
   tabletop (see page 81).

4 BRAZILIAN EDELWEISS (*Sinningia bullata*)
   The unusual crinkled foliage emerges from a
   visible bulb.

5 VARIEGATED MONSTERA
   Highly sought after and extremely rare, it makes
   for a table plant you can appreciate close up.

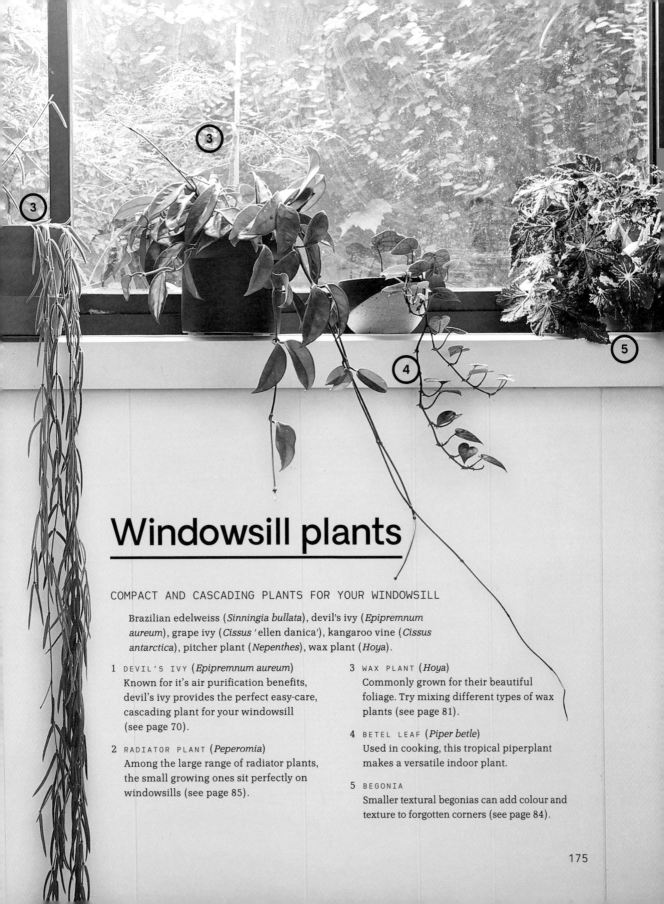

Windowsill plants

COMPACT AND CASCADING PLANTS FOR YOUR WINDOWSILL

Brazilian edelweiss (*Sinningia bullata*), devil's ivy (*Epipremnum aureum*), grape ivy (*Cissus* 'ellen danica'), kangaroo vine (*Cissus antarctica*), pitcher plant (*Nepenthes*), wax plant (*Hoya*).

1 DEVIL'S IVY (*Epipremnum aureum*)
Known for it's air purification benefits, devil's ivy provides the perfect easy-care, cascading plant for your windowsill (see page 70).

2 RADIATOR PLANT (*Peperomia*)
Among the large range of radiator plants, the small growing ones sit perfectly on windowsills (see page 85).

3 WAX PLANT (*Hoya*)
Commonly grown for their beautiful foliage. Try mixing different types of wax plants (see page 81).

4 BETEL LEAF (*Piper betle*)
Used in cooking, this tropical piperplant makes a versatile indoor plant.

5 BEGONIA
Smaller textural begonias can add colour and texture to forgotten corners (see page 84).

Shelf plants

Begonia, Chinese money plant (*Pilea peperomioides*), devil's ivy (*Epipremnum aureum*), Swiss cheese vine (*Monstera obliqua*), radiator plant (*Peperomia*), wax plant (*Hoya*) and plants from the *Philodendron* family.

1. WANDERING JEW (*Tradescantia pallida*)
   Wandering jew bears cascading purple and green leaves for a burst of colour.

2. SWISS CHEESE VINE (*Monstera obliqua*)
   The perforated foliage creates a beautiful specimen plant (see page 80).

3. *Philodendron family*
   Smaller philodendron species make great sculptural shelf plants.

4. WAX PLANT (*Hoya*)
   Wax plants happily cascade as they grow and will visually soften the edge of your shelf (see page 81).

5. PRAYER PLANT (*Maranta leuconeura*)
   If you are after an interesting plant, the 'praying' leaves of this variety move throughout the day (see page 73).

6. HEART-LEAF IVY (*Philodendron cordatum*)
   For a plainer leaf form, the heart-leaf ivy is another easy-care plant.

7. WATERMELON PEPEROMIA (*Peperomia argyreia*)
   Place these highly patterned and interesting plants at eye level, so you can enjoy their foliage (see page 85).

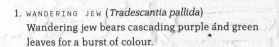

Plant and pot styling

As an architect and interior designer, I've always been inspired by nature. My love for indoor greenery brings together my profession and my passion and allows me to view the relationship between a plant and its pot more thoughtfully. Living with plants is about more than just the plant itself.

Styling your home with a plant in a complementary vessel helps to connect the plant with your interior and create a story. You don't have to settle for the standard black pot. There are numerous vessels and pots that can be sourced to keep your plants happy. If you're an amateur plant enthusiast, you might want to try self-watering pots while getting used to the world of indoor gardening. Once you have developed your gardening skills, you can start exploring handmade ceramic pots and vintage finds. I'm quite partial to the traditional terracotta pot and to supporting local ceramicists who offer a range of unique pots.

CRAFTING POTS

You can easily alter a standard pot to give it your own personality. The easiest and most effective way to do this is to paint it. Whether you choose to paint a pattern or simply a colour, this can lift your pot and change the look of your plant instantly.

Giving your plant a personality

Giving your plants personality doesn't have to be expensive. It's about choosing a combination of pots that will aesthetically add to your interior and keep your plants thriving. Where your plant will be positioned will guide you in choosing the right pot. For example, do you want the plant to hang or sit on a surface?

When I'm choosing a pot for my plant, I like to make the plant and pot contrast. Observe the plant's leaf foliage and texture.

STYLING TIP: If your plant has unusual foliage, choose a subtle pot that allows the plant to stand out. On the other hand, if the plant has plain foliage, pair it with a more interesting pot, perhaps one made by a local ceramicist.

181

Christina Symes & Jessica Stewart

We Are Triibe

LOCATION: SURRY HILLS, SYDNEY, AUSTRALIA
OCCUPATION: INTERIOR DESIGNERS
@WEARETRIIBE HTTP://WWW.WEARETRIIBE.COM

Design duo Christina and Jessica's distinctive style exemplifies a curated and refined use of indoor greenery. Coupled with considered plant styling by means of pots and planters, their design projects incorporate plants into interiors effectively, and beautifully.

HOW MANY PLANTS ARE IN YOUR COLLECTION?
CS: 26

JS: 6 at home, 14 in the office.

TELL US ABOUT YOUR DAILY ROUTINE AND HOW
PLANTS ARE INVOLVED.
CS: My day commences at sunrise. I am extremely
fortunate (and grateful) to be living in a two-bedroom
apartment that overlooks the ocean in Clovelly.
I haven't always lived on the eastern beaches.
Previously, I resided in the thick of inner Sydney,
which I thought is what I lived and breathed until I
began my day with a long ocean walk and taking in my
natural surroundings. I knew the sea change would
be good for me, however, the impact it has had on my
well-being, not to mention on the plants that made
the move with me, has been tenfold. They're putting
my height and complexion to shame with how much
they're growing and glowing in the new space.

The best part of my day is spent at the Triibe Concept
Studio. It is the opposite of a conventional office space
– it's currently painted a blush pink colour (including
the ceiling and window frames), and is bursting with
plants! We change the scheme every 6 months, [along
with] a full new curation of plants, depending on
the direction we take the space in. We believe that
plants can dictate the aesthetic. They also play a big
part in our daily wellbeing, as much as furniture and
products do.

JS: My daily routine is pretty varied, but [my morning]
always starts with a shower (sometimes with plants,
sometimes without, depending on which one needed
a water the night before!) and a walk along the beach
or the park near my house with my dog Rasta, and
continues with a coffee in hand ready to start the day.
It's really important for me to spend time in nature
every morning. Breathing in the fresh air and being
surrounded by trees and plants makes me feel happy
and revitalised, helping me to start my day on the
right foot.

WHAT DRAWS YOU TO PLANTS?
CS: Definitely their therapeutic qualities, and the
instant satisfaction I get from being surrounded by
nature – whether it's indoors or out.

JS: I love the way they look and how they can make you
feel. They make me happy, inside of my house and out.

WHAT IS YOUR FAVOURITE TYPE OF PLANT?
CS: It's difficult to round it down to one favourite; I
generally veer towards unusual, quirky plants – they
can add so much character to a space. However, if I
must choose, I have always loved and adored the *Pilea
peperomioides* plant, commonly known as the Chinese
money plant.

JS: Perhaps a *Philodendron*? But I don't know if I can
say I have a favourite. I'm definitely drawn to quirky,
strange and tropical plants.

HOW DID YOU LEARN ABOUT GARDENING?
CS: I am self-taught but still very much a novice
when it comes to plants; there has been a lot of trial
and error along the way. When sourcing, I consider
the location and temperature requirements prior to
purchasing and speak with the staff at the nurseries
to ensure I'm buying the right soil and to find out how
best to look after the plants throughout each season. I
generally just keep an eye on my plants each week and

can now tell if they look a little unhappy or require less or more sunlight, but that's taken practice! In saying so, I have overloved my plants in the past as well, either watering them too much or placing them in direct sunlight when they're a shade plant, so it's a real art that I respect.

JS: From my gorgeous dad. I was lucky to have grown up on a big block of land surrounded by farmland; it was full of fruit trees and beautiful plants that my dad had planted. Ever since I was a little kid, he has taught me things in the garden; he would show me how to grow plants in a veggie patch, or teach me how to prune and grow different plants from cuttings.

HOW DO YOU STYLE WITH PLANTS AND DO YOU HAVE ANY TIPS?
CS: Plants have the ability to give a space personality. Depending on the species you choose, it can really alter the feeling of the space. Plants are a great way to add height in areas, such as on top of consoles and shelving, or [to create impact] by using a large established tree in a living area.

Planters have a large impact on the space. It is therefore important to use ones that complement the overall colour scheme. They also can be a great styling item to use for contrast, for example, introducing a darker shade of the room's colour scheme or having an accent of colour.

JS: I love to style with plants, I think they make such a huge and easy impact in any space. I like to get an array of sizes so that I can style them in different areas, and I don't think you can ever really have too many.

I have a few tips when it comes to plants. My first tip would be not to be shy when opting for a large plant, as tall trees and vines can make a beautiful statement in your home. My second tip would be to invest in some beautiful ceramic planters as they can make such a big difference to how your plants look, and my final tip would be to wipe down the leaves of your plants every couple of weeks so that they don't get covered in dust and stay happy and healthy.

WERE YOU ALWAYS A GREEN THUMB?
CS: Unfortunately, I can't say I was. When I was younger my mum used to try to coerce me into the garden to help and I would tell her it was so boring! But I still remember to this day her saying to me 'you just wait, I never used to like it either but you will grow to love it' ... And sure enough, she was right.

JS: I think so! I've managed to keep my plants alive for as long as I can remember.

WHAT DO YOU LOVE ABOUT HOUSEPLANTS WHEN IT COMES TO INTERIORS?
CS: I truly believe plants are the heart and soul of a space, without them a space can feel incomplete, lifeless and, sometimes, disjointed. Our home is our sanctuary, and I love that plants play a huge role in creating our happy space; they are the final touch that ties everything together and they help lift the whole energy in each room.

JS: I love how they can completely transform a space. A couple of years ago, a friend who had just moved into a house after living overseas had a limited budget to buy styling items with. She asked me what I thought she should buy to make it feel like a home.

I told her to fill her space with as many plants as she could, because, in my eyes, the simple task of adding plants to your space can instantly make your house feel like a home.

WHEN CHOOSING A POT, WHAT DO YOU CONSIDER?

CS: I usually gravitate towards pots with an organic shape and finish. A play on heights, size and finishes always helps create a bit more balance, especially when working with multiple plants in one space. I also like to ensure the colour of the pot is considered and complements the rest of the scheme and furnishings in the space.

JS: I can't go past a beautiful hand-thrown ceramic planter, and I always consider the colours that I choose to make sure that they complement the interior that they're being placed in. They also always need to come with a drip-tray, which makes it easier to water them.

Index

N

naming conventions 31
neem oil pesticide recipe 125
Nepenthes 40, 158, 175
nerve plant 48
new leaves too small 128
non-toxic plants 27
nutrients 38, 44, 47
   problems related to 129

O

office/desk 162–5
organic fungicide recipe 125
Oxalis 110

P

panda plant 49
paper plant 40
peace lily 23, 37, 40, 46, 49, **75**, 117, 144, 152,
   158, 163, 170
peacock plant 49, **90**, 142, 149, 170, 172
Peperomia 27, 40, 46, 48, **85**, 112, 113, 115,
   149, 172, 175, 176
   argyreia 177
pesticides, homemade 124–5
pests and control methods 132–3
pets and plants 27
Philodendron 40, 46, 61, 111, 114, 144, 152,
   176, 177
   bipennifolium 49
   bipinnatifidum 48
   cordatum 48, 142, 177
   'red emerald' 49
Pilea 46, 113, 116
   cadierei 27, 48
   peperomioides 40, 49, **86**, 149, 172, 176
pinch pruning 58
Piper betle 175
pitcher plant 40, 158, 175
plant maintenance 51, 123
plant naming conventions 31
plant people 32–3, 62–5, 118–19, 134–5, 182–5
plant problems 122–3
   diseases 130–1
   pests 132–3
   related to light 126
   related to nutrients 129
   related to temperature 128
   related to water 127
plant ties 28
plastic pots 52, 53, 107
Platycerium 48

pots
   choosing 52–3, 107
   correct size 54
   for soil and seed propagation 107
   for styling 179–81
potting medium 44
potting mixes 44, 46
potting on 103
powdery mildew 131
prayer plant 27, 40, 48, **73**, 149, 172, 177
propagating mix 46
propagating vessels 103
   for soil and seed propagation 107
   for water propagation 104
propagation 103
   methods 110–17
   when to propagate 103
pruning your plants 58–9, 61

Q

queen of hearts 40, 48, **76**, 142, 144, 149, 158, 171

R

radiator plant 27, 40, 48, **85**, 142, 149, 172, 175
rainforest palms 40
reception areas 166–7
red emerald philodendron 49
repotting 44, 54
   how to repot 56–7
   pot size 54
   when to repot 54
Rhapis 166
root rot 31, 127
rooting mediums 103
rubber plant 37, 40, 48, 61, **79**, 144, 152, 166, 170
runners 116

S

saddle-leaved plant 48
Saintpaulia 27, 49, 112
scale 133
Schefflera 40, 48, 144, 170
secateur pruning 58, 59
secateurs 28
seed propagation 110
   vessels for 107
sensitive plants 49
Sinningia 46
   bullata 172, 175
slow growth 126, 129
slow-release fertiliser 47
small handmade ceramic pots 107

Thank you

To the growers, collectors and crazy plant people I have met along this journey, I sincerely thank you and look forward to continuing this plant adventure together.

My plant journey began with a bond between my grandparents, parents and me. My family have always been the most supportive and loving mentors, to whom I owe my life. I also owe them the biggest thanks for allowing me to embrace what I love in life.

To my family and friends, who have given us an infinite amount of support and positivity, we could not have done this without you. The Plant Society would not be as fulfilling or full of laughs and smiles without your support.

This book would not have been as fun without Bobby and Steven Clark, Anna Rozen and Taj Darvall, and Matt Curtis and Tom Robertson architects allowing us to turn their homes and offices upside down. Thank you! A huge thank you to Anna Collett and Melissa Kayser for being such an amazing support while working on this book. I would also like to thank editor Michael Ryan for his attention to detail, photographer Armelle Habib for capturing every moment as I had imagined it in my mind, and designer Andy Warren for beautifully portraying my journey onto paper. I couldn't have asked for better collaborators!

To Heather Nette King, who held me by the shoulders when we first met and told me to get ready for what was to come. Thanks for allowing me to bounce so many ideas off you and for providing me with your undying support, not to mention allowing us into your home.

A special thanks to Nathan Smith for being the best partner in crime one could ever wish for. There aren't many people who would happily support all of my wildest plant ideas as well as live in a real-life indoor rainforest! I owe the world to you!

About the author

Jason Chongue is a Melbourne-based architect, interior designer and plant cultivator.

His career has been shaped by a range of unique design and gardening experiences. At 19, Jason launched his design career as head visual merchandiser at Koko Black while completing his Masters of Architecture in Melbourne, London and New York. After graduating, he worked with architectural firms large and small across the retail, hospitality and residential sectors. Currently, Jason works on a range of architectural, interior design and styling projects.

Unambiguously passionate about design, he also has an innate love of cultivating indoor greenery and has been a plant cultivator for as long as he can remember, growing a range of plants with his family, especially his grandmother. His love for all things green has led him to collect a huge number of rare and unusual plants sourced through long-nurtured relationships with other growers.

In August 2016, he launched The Plant Society (www.theplantsociety.com.au/ @theplantsocietyau) with his partner, Nathan Smith. Together they promote positive and open conversations about gardening and greenery. Their passion lies in providing a supportive social network for gardeners of all levels. The Plant Society's 'Plant Social' events bring together growers and plant enthusiasts to informally talk about plant-care tips or growing challenges and build awareness about gardening in small spaces.

Jason's mammoth plant collection and unique interiors were discovered by *The Planthunter* via his Instagram (@jasonchongue) in 2016. He has also appeared in *The Design Files*, *Sunday Life* and the *Sydney Morning Herald,* and been noted as 'one of five plant-obsessed Instagram accounts to follow' by Nine News and one of '10 Instagrammers from Australia and New Zealand to follow' by Design*Sponge.

Jason believes the skills of gardening have skipped a generation, which has opened a gap for educating the younger generation about simple skills and knowledge relating to indoor gardening. He is passionate about gaining knowledge from established growers to preserve the history of plants, both in Australia and internationally.

Published in 2017 by Hardie Grant Books,
an imprint of Hardie Grant Publishing

Hardie Grant Books (Melbourne)
Building 1, 658 Church Street
Richmond, Victoria 3121

Hardie Grant Books (London)
5th & 6th Floors
52-54 Southwark Street
London SE1 1UN

hardiegrantbooks.com

A catalogue record for this
book is available from the
National Library of Australia

Plant Society
ISBN 978 1 74379 343 5

10 9 8 7 6 5 4

Commissioning Editor: Melissa Kayser
Managing Editor: Marg Bowman
Project Editor: Anna Collett
Editor: Michael Ryan
Designer: Andy Warren
Photographer: Armelle Habib
Illustrator: Astred Hicks
Stylist: Jason Chongue
Production Manager:Todd Rechner

Colour reproduction by Splitting Image Colour Studio
Printed in China by Leo Paper Product. LTD

Special thanks to Bauwerk @bauwerkcolour https://www.bauwerk.com.au,
Halcyon Lake @halcyonlake http://halcyonlake.com, Ivy Muse @ivymuse_melb
https://ivymuse.com.au, In Bed @inbedstore https://inbedstore.com,
Mark Tuckey @mark_tuckey http://www.marktuckey.com.au and G-Lux @glluuxx
https://www.g-lux.com.au for generously providing props for the photoshoot as
well as for their constant support.